Anne Manning

The Maiden and Married Life of Mary Powell

Anne Manning

The Maiden and Married Life of Mary Powell

ISBN/EAN: 9783337017637

Printed in Europe, USA, Canada, Australia, Japan

Cover: Foto ©ninafisch / pixelio.de

More available books at **www.hansebooks.com**

MARY POWELL

AND ITS SEQUEL

DEBORAH'S DIARY

By the same Author

In crown 8vo, uniform with this volume

Each Volume with an Introduction by the Rev. W. H. HUTTON, B.D., and 26 Illustrations by JOHN JELLICOE and HERBERT RAILTON

The Household of Sir Thos. More

Cherry & Violet:
A Tale of the Great Plague

The many other interesting works of this author will be published from time to time uniformly with the above.

Illustrations by John Jellicoe & Herbert Railton

Introduction by The Rev. W. H. Hutton

London
John C. Nimmo
·MDCCCXCVIII·

THE
MAIDEN & MARRIED LIFE OF
MARY POWELL

(Afterwards Mistress Milton)

AND THE SEQUEL THERETO

DEBORAH'S DIARY

WITH AN INTRODUCTION BY

THE REV. W. H. HUTTON, B.D.
FELLOW OF S. JOHN'S COLLEGE, OXFORD

AND TWENTY-SIX ILLUSTRATIONS BY
JOHN JELLICOE AND HERBERT RAILTON

LONDON
JOHN C. NIMMO
NEW YORK: CHARLES SCRIBNER'S SONS
MDCCCXCVIII

Printed by BALLANTYNE, HANSON & Co.
At the Ballantyne Press

LIST OF ILLUSTRATIONS

From Drawings by JOHN JELLICOE *and* HERBERT RAILTON.

AT FOREST HILL.
    Drawn by JOHN JELLICOE *and* HERBERT RAILTON   *Frontispiece*

TITLE-PAGE.   PAGE
    Designed by HERBERT RAILTON iii

HEADPIECE.
    Drawn by HERBERT RAILTON 1

AT SHEEPSCOTE.
    Drawn by JOHN JELLICOE *and* HERBERT RAILTON *To face* 4

"HE OFFERED ME SOME WILD FLOWERS."
    Drawn by JOHN JELLICOE 7

THE BOWLING-GREEN AT FOREST HILL.
    Drawn by JOHN JELLICOE *and* HERBERT RAILTON *To face* 26

"MR. MILTON LOITERED WITH ME ON THE TERRACE."
    Drawn by JOHN JELLICOE *and* HERBERT RAILTON ,, 30

"I WENT DOWN WITH ROBIN AND KATE TO THE FISH-PONDS."
    Drawn by JOHN JELLICOE *and* HERBERT RAILTON ,, 40

List of Illustrations

	PAGE
"STRANGE DIVERTING CRIES IN THE STREETS."	
Drawn by JOHN JELLICOE . . . *To face* 62	
"TENDERLY BOUND UP HIS HAND."	
Drawn by JOHN JELLICOE 85	
"AT SQUIRE PAICE'S GRAND DINNER."	
Drawn by JOHN JELLICOE *and* HERBERT RAILTON *To face* 106	
"THEN MR. AGNEW CAME AND SATE ON A FLAT TOMBSTONE."	
Drawn by JOHN JELLICOE *and* HERBERT RAILTON ,, 138	
"THE RARE EVENT OF A DINNER GUEST."	
Drawn by JOHN JELLICOE 166	
"THEY PAUSED IN SURPRISE AT SEEING MILTON ASLEEP."	
Drawn by JOHN JELLICOE . . . . *To face* 182	
"THREW IT FORTHE WITH A PAIR OF TONGS."	
Drawn by JOHN JELLICOE 212	
"THUS I REMAINED, AGONIZED IN TEARS."	
Drawn by JOHN JELLICOE . . . *To face* 216	
MILTON'S HOUSE, BARBICAN.	
Drawn by HERBERT RAILTON . ,, 218	
"SOME POORE FOLK TO RELIEVE AND CONSOLE."	
Drawn by JOHN JELLICOE . . . 232	
BUNHILL FIELDS (*Frontispiece to* " Deborah's Diary").	
Drawn by HERBERT RAILTON . *To face* 238	

		PAGE
"OUT COMES A VOLLEY OF POETRY."		
Drawn by JOHN JELLICOE.	. . .	246
"YET FORTY DAYS."		
Drawn by JOHN JELLICOE.	. . .	273
"I TOOK THE VOLUME TO HIS SHOP."		
Drawn by JOHN JELLICOE *and* HERBERT RAILTON	*To face*	286
"HOUSES PADLOCKED AND SHUTTERED."		
Drawn by JOHN JELLICOE *and* HERBERT RAILTON	,,	294
MILTON'S COTTAGE AT CHALFONT.		
Drawn by HERBERT RAILTON.	. ,,	296
"THROWING HIS ARM ABOUT ME."		
Drawn by JOHN JELLICOE.	.	299
"NO HARM, I PROMISE YOU, MASTER."		
Drawn by JOHN JELLICOE.	. . .	314
"HE POURS FORTH THE FULL TIDE OF MELODY ON HIS ORGAN."		
Drawn by JOHN JELLICOE *and* HERBERT RAILTON	*To face*	318

Introduction

THE republication of "The Household of Sir Thomas More" and "Cherry and Violet" has aroused much interest in the personality of their author. Two years ago, from a brief correspondence in *Notes and Queries*, it might have seemed as if she had been entirely forgotten; but since her books have attained a new popularity some interesting accounts of her retired life have reached me through the kindness of friends.

She is remembered at Reigate as a tall, thin lady with black hair, an aquiline nose, and a bright colour. She lived very quietly, and was considered "old-fashioned" by the few who knew her intimately. She is described as at times bitter in her satire; and in her later years, when she was obliged to spend much time on her couch from ill-health, " rather hard " in voice. Her literary activity, it is clear, must have been very great, and she was a wide reader in all directions; but her powers, it would seem, remained for a long time unnoticed; and those who knew her reserved character and somewhat stiff manner expressed astonishment when they discovered that it was she who had written the charming book of which every one was talking, " The Maiden and Married Life of Mary Powell," which has always been the most popular of her works. In opinion she was a stout English Churchwoman, of the type, perhaps, which has been dubbed " high and dry," constant in attendance at daily services, correct, restrained, sincere. Of her genuine homeliness there can be no more doubt than of her real piety. One who knew her speaks of her as "a very gentle, quiet lady," says that a book of quaint cookery recipes in her writing, which she gave to a friend, is still in existence, and tells that she once said " she liked darning stockings, as when so employed she could think out her books." She was very kind to young literary aspirants, and one to whom she was much attached writes : " Her loss to me as a dear friend, as well as a kind, judicious, and actively helpful literary adviser, was very great."

These few memories are helpful in fixing an impression of one whom we should be glad that lovers of *genre*-painting in literature should not forget. The two stories which are now combined in this volume possess all her characteristic merits. It was a happy inspiration that set Miss Manning's imagination to work upon the life of the great Puritan poet. There is a contrast which no student can fail to have observed between the charm of his character, in its purity, gentleness, and eager love of truth, and the circumstances of his relations to those most near to him in kindred. It is not difficult to see that, apart from the unhappy fate which seems often to pursue men of genius in their married life, there were reasons for his sorrows in the bitterness of party feeling which accompanied the strength of his convictions. Married life, we are told, must be always something of a compromise, and of compromise Milton was utterly abhorrent. The contrasts of his character and his life are reflected in his work. Who could believe that the same hand wrote "Il Penseroso" and "Eikonoklastes"? With all the softness of face and sweetness of imagination there is a certain hardness, even harshness, that will not be denied utterance, and the middle period of his life is that in which this harshness finds its chief expression. His personality, indeed, lacks a perfect harmony, and it is this, though it be temerarious to assert it, which makes him fail to reach the perfection of a religious poet. Magnificence in conception, profundity in thought, imagination, reverence, truth, he has all these, and yet—if I may repeat with emphasis a statement which has been severely criticised—he has not that note of absolute sincerity and self-abandonment which makes Christina Rossetti supreme in spiritual verse. He felt, perhaps, the two sides of life too keenly: with all his cloistered sympathies, he dwelt too much in the world, and when political and ecclesiastical warfare had soured his spirit, he never recovered the exquisite harmony of his earlier days. Landor has said very truly that in "Paradise Regained" he "seems to be subject to strange hallucinations of the ear; he who before had greatly excelled all poets of all ages in the science and display of harmony." I will complete the passage, for it may serve to correct my own less enthusiastic judgment. "And if in his last poem we exhibit his deficiencies, surely we never shall be accused of disrespect or irreverence to this immortal man. It may be doubted whether the Creator ever created one altogether so great; taking into our view at once (as much indeed as can at once be taken into it) his manly virtues, his superhuman genius, his zeal for truth, for true piety, true freedom, his eloquence in displaying it, his contempt of personal power, his glory and exaltation in his country's." Alas! his greatness is not untouched by his misfortunes; for indeed it is difficult for an unbiassed moral judgment to believe that his relations with his wife and with his daughters were entirely the succession of miseries utterly undeserved. However this may be, it is the rare merit of Miss Manning's sensitive imagination that, in " The Maiden and Married Life of Mary Powell " and " Deborah's Diary," while she has caught our sympathies for her heroines, she has never made us lose our love for Milton.

The historical facts on which these stories have been based are perhaps too familiar to need restatement; yet they may be briefly summarised. In 1643

John Milton was thirty-four. He was well known in high circles of literature and society: he had travelled, studied, and thought. There was no living Englishman, it might be said, who had a higher ideal in life or a higher performance in literature. He had already reached, in "Lycidas," "the high-water mark of English poesy and of his own production." But he was also already a keen politician, an eager supporter of the party which felt most strongly against the king and the Cavaliers.

It was then, about Whitsuntide, as his nephew tells us, " that he took a journey, nobody about him certainly knowing the reason, or that it was any more than a journey of recreation. After a month's stay, home he returns a married man that went out a bachelor: his wife being Mary, the eldest daughter of Mr. Richard Powell, then a Justice of Peace, of Forest Hill, near Shotover, in Oxfordshire." The county he knew already, and, it is most likely, the family. His father was born at Stanton St. John, the next village to Forest Hill: and Richard Powell, the father of his bride, was his debtor in the sum of £500. That Milton, a marked man, should have gone at this time so near to the Royalist camp at Oxford, and that his marriage should have been, as it seems, so hastily arranged, are other points in a mysterious story. The young bride went to lodgings in Aldersgate Street with her husband. After a month her friends at home "made earnest suit, by letter, to have her company the remaining part of the summer." She went, and she did not return at Michaelmas, as Milton had desired. Letters were unanswered, and a messenger was "dismissed with some sort of contempt." Were the faults all on one side? At any rate it is certain that before his wife had left him Milton had begun to write a pamphlet on "The Doctrine and Discipline of Divorce," in which the freedom of a husband to part from his wife "for lack of a fit and matchable conversation" is vehemently asserted, though no such freedom is allowed to the "weaker vessel."

Professor Masson, Mr. Mark Pattison, Dr. S. R. Gardiner, Mr. Leslie Stephen, have sounded the depths that cover the strange history of Milton's marriage, and have said many sage things, but (through no fault of their own) perhaps not one that is convincing. Where these grave persons admit their difficulties it may be a relief to turn to the delicate art with which Miss Manning has told the story, simply and with a true imaginative sympathy for a young girl's inevitable difficulties in the first weeks of married life. Milton, in later days, said that "the bashful muteness of a virgin may ofttimes hide all the unliveliness and natural sloth which is really unfit for conversation." It is very likely that he did not recognise, as those of poetic temper are very loth to do, that a man of thirty-four is not still in his first youth, while a girl of seventeen has not really reached womanhood; and there was in his soul, with all its sweetness and purity, an underlying harshness of temper.

> " God's universal law
> Gave to man despotic power
> Over his female in due awe,
> Nor from that right to part an hour."

Those are lines as bitter as any that his pen wrote in prose. But happily the spirit which wrote the Divorce treatises, and which even suggested that the banished wife might find a successor in his home, was not unquenchable. Before two years were out, in the house of friends, the young girl, not yet nineteen, threw herself at her husband's feet and was taken back.

They had four children, Anne, born 1646; Mary, 1648; John (who died an infant), 1651; Deborah, 1652; and the wife died in the year of the birth of her youngest child.

In 1656 Milton married Catherine Woodcock, who died in February 1658. In February 1663 he married Elizabeth Minshull, who lived till 1727.

All accounts point to much family disagreement, and Milton in the year of his death (1674), spoke to his brother of his "undutiful children." Yet here again the faults were not all on one side. The girls were taught to read aloud in five or six languages, without being allowed to learn the meaning of what they read. Only Deborah was taught Latin, and she became her father's amanuensis. Before he died they were all sent out to learn embroidery in gold and silver, that they might earn their living. Mary died unmarried, the others married poorly. It is a story even more pathetic than the first episode of misunderstanding, and it seems clear that it lasted to the end. Only Deborah appears in later days to have entertained a kindly memory of her father. Two years before her death, when she was sixty-three, she was shown a drawing without being told for whom it was meant. "O Lord!" she said at once, "that is the picture of my father," and she stroked down the hair of her forehead with "just so my father wore his hair."

Miss Manning happily seized upon a year which we may hope may have been brighter than the rest of the poet's evil days, and something of her picture of the country retreat must certainly be true. It is not likely that the observant Ellwood would have failed to record it, if there had been much family disagreement in the house he so often visited. He was long Milton's friend and pupil, and the formal quaintness of his "History written by Himself" adds not a little to the pleasantness of the picture which imagination may draw of the brighter side of these last years. Ellwood himself suffered persecution for his opinions, and he could feel for the Puritan poet who had once been Latin secretary.

The words on which Miss Manning founded the main story of her "Deborah's Diary" are these: "Some little time before I went to Aylesbury prison," says Ellwood, "I was desired by my quondam master, Milton, to take a house for him in the neighbourhood, where I dwelt, that he might go out of the city, for the safety of himself and his family, the pestilence then growing hot in London. I took a pretty box for him in Giles Chalfont, a mile from me, of which I gave him notice; and intended to have waited on him, and seen him well settled in it, but was prevented by that imprisonment. But now being released and returned home, I soon made a visit to him, to welcome him into the country. After some common discourses had passed between us, he called for a manuscript of his; which being brought he delivered to me, bidding me take it home with me, and read it at my leisure; and when I had so done, return it to him with my judgment thereupon. When I came home, and had set myself to read it, I found it was that excellent poem which he entitled 'Paradise Lost.' After I had, with the best attention, read it through, I made him another visit, and returned him his book, with due acknowledgment of the favour he had done me in communicating it to me. He asked me how I liked it and what I thought of it, which I modestly but freely told him, and after some further discourse about it, I pleasantly said to him, 'Thou hast said much here of "Paradise Lost," but what hast thou to say of "Paradise Found"'? He made me no answer, but sat some time in a muse; then brake off that discourse, and fell upon another subject. After the sickness was over, and the city well cleansed and become safely habitable again, he returned thither. And when afterwards I went to wait on him there, which I seldom failed of doing whenever my occasions drew me to London, he showed me his second poem, called 'Paradise Regained,' and in a pleasant tone said to me, 'This is owing to you, for you put it into my head by the question you put to me at Chalfont, which before I had not thought of.'"

The passage is a famous one, and we do

not need here any comment on it, save that which Miss Manning has herself supplied. She has woven too into her imaginary diary, with a singular skill, the facts that are known as to the stepmother, the daughters, and the servant, with just those touches of fancy that may make the picture live.

The two stories are now, I think, very happily reprinted together. "Mary Powell" first appeared in 1851, and went through many editions. "Deborah's Diary" was published in 1860. We have now the advantage of the skill of Mr. Railton and Mr. Jellicoe, who know how to make the times and the men live again to-day.

I have seen the drawings from which the illustrations for this book are to be printed, and I cannot but feel that both artists have experienced to the full the attraction of the subject. To Mr. Jellicoe has been given the difficult duty of drawing the Milton whose portrait we all know, and his young bride, of whose fair face we have no record. He has had to show us too the old blind man dictating to his daughter; and it could not have been done more happily. To Mr. Railton it has fallen to sketch, as it was in the seventeenth century, the one house still standing where Milton lived, and the harder task to image the places which, with little or no visible survival of his days, we still associate with his memory: and so he has given us these delightful pictures of Forest Hill, and the Barbican, and Bunhill Fields, instinct with true feeling for the past.

The chief scenes of these two stories are well worth a visit. Forest Hill stands about four miles from Oxford, a short way from the main road to London, and up a sharp ascent—a pleasant walk or ride, now as no doubt in Milton's day, for scholars of the university. The old manor-house, which Miss Manning no doubt had seen, was pulled down in 1854. In 1851 it was thus described in "Impressions of England," by the Rev. A.

Cleveland Coxe, rector of Christ Church, Baltimore : —

"It presents the remains of a much larger house; but, even in its reduced dimensions, is quite sufficient for a comfortable farmer. Still the rose, the sweet-briar, and the eglantine are redolent beneath its casements; the cock at the barn-door may be seen from any of its windows; and doubtless, the barn itself is the very one in which the shadowy flail of Robin Goodfellow threshed all night, to earn his bowl of cream. In the house itself, we were received by the farmer's daughter, who looked like the 'neat-handed Phillis' herself, although her accomplishments were by no means those of a rustic maiden, for she had evidently entered fully into the spirit of the place, and imbued herself with that of the poetry in no mean degree. We were indebted to her for the most courteous reception, and were conducted by her into several apartments of the house, concerning all of which she was able to converse very intelligently. In the kitchen, with its vast hearth and overhanging chimney, we discovered tokens of the good living for which the old manor-house was no doubt famous in its day; and in its floor was a large stone, said to have been removed from a room now destroyed, which was the poet's study.

"The garden, in its massive wall, ornamented gateway, and an old sun-dial, retains some trace of its manorial dignities in former times; when the maiden Mary sat in her bower thinking of her inspired lover; or when perchance the runaway wife sighed and wept over a letter brought by the post, commanding Mistress Milton to return to her duty in a dark corner of London. . . .

"Our fair conductress next called our attention to an outhouse, now degraded to the office of domestic brewing, . . . and in proof of the nobler office to which it had been originally designed, she pointed out the remains of old *pargetting*, or ornamented plaster-work, in its gables."

All this is now swept away, save a

wall or two partly used in the construction of the substantial farm-house built in a time of agricultural prosperity. In and about the farm-yard stand many walnut trees, some of great age; and the farm buildings, too, are old. Hard by in a field is a spring, arched over with strong masonry. Here, as the romantic American traveller thought, John Milton may have tasted of the pure water. Several thatched houses in the village should have been seen by Mary Powell as she walked to meet Master Milton along the ridge that stretches, with distant views of the Chilterns, towards the deserted village watering-place of Brill. But the clearest memories of King Charles's days come from the church, set high on the hill amid ancient yews. Little country girls, with fresh beaming faces, hang over the old grey wall as we climb the ascent. So, hat in hand, would our heroine watch for her poet's coming, and surely she was no brighter or more happy than are they. A quaint old holly, covered with berries now at midsummer, stands by the gate. The high bell-cot, clothed in ivy, is the church's great distinction; but it is all, in spite of the cruelties of Sir Gilbert Scott, a pretty piece of restful antiquity. It was consecrated, the records tell us, in 1273, and it bears the name of Saint Nicholas. In Laud's day it was furbished up, in the spirit which made the archbishop write: "It is true, the inward worship of the heart is the great service of God, and no service acceptable without it; but the external worship of God in His church is the great witness to the world, that our heart stands right in that service of God." The great oak beam across the chancel arch, with its inscription "C. R., 1630," is a memorial of this restoration. But these are after all but slight survivals of the times of Mistress Mary Powell; the more abiding memory attaches to the tranquillity of the verdant slopes and the lanes, with their hedges full of sweet-briar, that stretch down towards Oxford. One could not find a sweeter setting for the youth of the damsel who was to be John Milton's bride.

It is a different thought which brings us, with "Deborah's Diary," to the cottage at Chalfont, and the old age of the blind poet. There are few prettier English villages than that in which Thomas Ellwood found a lodging for his "quondam master." It lies hidden in the heart of numberless beech-woods, off the track of the great highroads. Now it can be easily approached by the Metropolitan Railway, which has a station about three miles off; and, indeed, the village itself is little more than twenty miles from the Marble Arch. None the less is it still buried in seclusion, and everything that is old here shows a loving care. A charming little pamphlet tells the story of the village very happily, and is proof, if any were wanted beyond the church itself, of the rector's labours and knowledge. For pilgrims who visit the place because it contains the only house still standing in which Milton lived, there are yet many other sights which should not be passed by. The church, with its fine brasses and monuments, its two beautiful windows by Mr. Kempe, and its whole air of true " decency and order," has preserved a memory of the poet, though, indeed, it is like enough that he never crossed its door. The village green, the old red-roofed cottages, the pond, the fine trees, give many pretty pictures as you mount the gentle slope that leads to the house which gives Chalfont its fame in two continents. A very simple homely dwelling it is, part of a row of others still inhabited, and not a little altered. The cottage itself is, one is glad to see, not entirely given over to the craze for a museum, and with its white-washed parlour, stocked with old oak, and dignified with framed documents that tell the house's history, and books of Milton's writing and his times, it has yet some dwellers who serve to give it a homely air of use. In the low room to the left hand of the door you may fancy Milton sitting with his leg over the chair-arm, dictating to his daughter, or you may close your eyes and think you hear him upstairs tapping against the wall till Deborah comes in her night-cotes to take down his "volley of poetry." There is the garden, too, with its quaint old flowers, just such another as Anne Hathaway's at Shottery, with a hedge that Mistress Milton may have set her clothes on while her husband sat in his straight chair under shade of the little porch. It is pleasant that the abiding memory of the poet should belong to a village so sweet and unharmed as this.

All round are the Quaker memorials of the Penns, the Penningtons, and stiff Thomas Ellwood. The parish registers have record of the deaths of the great Penn himself, of his second wife, and of Milton's Quaker pupil, and in the parish is the famous burying-place of Jordans, where they rest. The village has its wider interests, its records of Marlborough's chaplain and secret messenger, of Captain Cook and his friend Sir Hugh

Palliser, a fiery British admiral. But the memory of Milton will outlive all these. Is it too much to say that Miss Manning, in her simple way, did not a little to preserve it?

W. H. HUTTON.

THE GREAT HOUSE, BURFORD,
 Visitation of the B.V.M., 1897.

JOURNALL

Forest Hill, Oxon, May 1st, 1643.

SEVENTEENTH Birthdaye. A Gypsie Woman at the Gate woulde faine have tolde my Fortune; but *Mother* chased her away, saying she had doubtlesse harboured in some of the low Houses

Houses in *Oxford*, and mighte bring us the Plague. Coulde have cried for Vexation; she had promised to tell me the Colour of my Husband's Eyes; but *Mother* says she believes I shall never have one, I am soe sillie. *Father* gave me a gold Piece. Dear *Mother* is chafed, methinks, touching this Debt of five hundred Pounds, which *Father* says he knows not how to pay. Indeed, he sayd, overnighte, his whole personal Estate amounts to but five hundred Pounds, his Timber and Wood to four hundred more, or thereabouts; and the Tithes and Messuages of *Whateley* are no great Matter, being mortgaged for about as much moore, and he hath lent Sights of Money to them that won't pay, so 'tis hard to be thus prest. Poor *Father!* 'twas good of him to give me this gold Piece.

May

May 2nd.

COUSIN *Rose* married to Master *Roger Agnew*. Present, *Father*, *Mother*, and *Brother* of *Rose*. *Father*, *Mother*, *Dick*, *Bob*, *Harry*, and I; Squire *Paice* and his Daughter *Audrey;* an olde Aunt of Master *Roger's*, and one of his Cousins, a stiffe-backed Man with large Eares, and such a long Nose! Cousin *Rose* looked bewtifulle—pitie so faire a Girl should marry so olde a Man—'tis thoughte he wants not manie Years of fifty.

May 7th.

NEW Misfortunes in the Poultrie Yarde. Poor *Mother's* Loyalty cannot stand the Demands for her best Chickens, Ducklings, &c., for the Use of his Majesty's Officers since the King hath beene in *Oxford*. She accuseth my *Father* of having beene

beene wonne over by a few faire Speeches to be more of a Royalist than his natural Temper inclineth him to; which, of course, he will not admit.

May 8th.

WHOLE Day taken up in a Visit to *Rose*, now a Week married, and growne quite matronlie already. We reached *Sheepscote* about an Hour before Noone. A long, broade, strait Walke of green Turf, planted with Hollyoaks, Sunflowers, &c., and some earlier Flowers alreadie in Bloom, led up to the rusticall Porch of a truly farm-like House, with low gable Roofs, a long lattice Window on either Side the Doore, and three Casements above. Such, and no more, is *Rose's* House! But she is happy, for she came running forthe, soe soone as she hearde *Clover's* Feet, and helped me from my Saddle all smiling, tho' she had not expected to see us. We had Curds and Creame;

Creame; and she wished it were the Time of Strawberries, for she sayd they had large Beds; and then my *Father* and the Boys went forthe to looke for Master *Agnew*. Then *Rose* took me up to her Chamber, singing as she went; and the long, low Room was sweet with Flowers. Sayd I, "*Rose*, to be Mistress of this pretty "Cottage, 'twere hardlie amisse to marry a "Man as olde as Master *Roger*." "Olde!" quoth she, "deare *Moll*, you must not "deeme him olde; why, he is but forty- "two; and am not I twenty-three?" She lookt soe earneste and hurte, that I coulde not but falle a laughing.

May 8th.

MOTHER gone to *Sandford*. She hopes to get Uncle *John* to lend *Father* this Money. *Father* says she may *try*. 'Tis harde to dis- courage her with an ironi- calle Smile, when she is doing alle she can, and more than manie Women woulde, to to help *Father* in his Difficultie; but suche, she sayth somewhat bitterlie, is the lot of our Sex. She bade *Father* mind that she had brought him three thousand Pounds, and askt what had come of them. Answered; helped to fille the Mouths of nine healthy Children, and stop the Mouth of an easie Husband; soe, with a Kiss, made it up. I have the Keys, and am left Mistresse of alle, to my greate Contentment; but the Children clamour for Sweetmeats, and *Father* sayth, " Remem-" ber, *Moll*, Discretion is the better part " of Valour."

After *Mother* had left, went into the Paddock, to feed the Colts with Bread; and while they were putting their Noses into *Robin's* Pockets, *Dick* brought out the two Ponies, and set me on one of them, and we had a mad Scamper through the Meadows and down the Lanes; I leading. Just at the Turne of *Holford's Close*, came shorte upon a Gentleman walking under the Hedge, clad in a sober, genteel Suit, and of most beautifulle Countenance, with
Hair

Hair like a Woman's, of a lovely pale brown, long and silky, falling over his Shoulders. I nearlie went over him, for

Clover's hard Forehead knocked agaynst his Chest; but he stoode it like a Rock; and lookinge firste at me and then at *Dick*, he smiled

smiled and spoke to my Brother, who seemed to know him, and turned about and walked by us, sometimes stroaking *Clover's* shaggy Mane. I felte a little ashamed; for *Dick* had sett me on the Poney just as I was, my Gown somewhat too shorte for riding: however, I drewe up my Feet and let *Clover* nibble a little Grasse, and then got rounde to the neare Side, our new Companion stille between us. He offered me some wild Flowers, and askt me theire Names; and when I tolde them, he sayd I knew more than he did, though he accounted himselfe a prettie fayre Botaniste: and we went on thus, talking of the Herbs and Simples in the Hedges; and I sayd how prettie some of theire Names were, and that, methought, though Adam had named alle the Animals in Paradise, perhaps Eve had named alle the Flowers. He lookt earnestlie at me, on this, and muttered "prettie." Then *Dick* askt of him News from *London*, and he spoke, methought, reservedlie; ever and anon turning his bright,

bright, thoughtfulle Eyes on me. At length, we parted at the Turn of the Lane.

I askt *Dick* who he was, and he told me he was one Mr. *John Milton*, the Party to whom *Father* owed five hundred Pounds. He was the Sonne of a *Buckinghamshire* Gentleman, he added, well connected, and very scholarlike, but affected towards the Parliament. His Grandsire, a zealous Papiste, formerly lived in *Oxon*, and disinherited the Father of this Gentleman for abjuring the *Romish* Faith.

When I found how faire a Gentleman was *Father's* Creditor, I became the more interested in deare *Mother's* Successe.

May 13*th.*

DICK began to harpe on another Ride to *Sheepscote* this Morning, and persuaded *Father* to let him have the bay Mare, soe he and I started at aboute Ten o' the Clock. Arrived at Master *Agnew's* Doore,

Doore, found it open, no one in Parlour or Studdy; soe *Dick* tooke the Horses rounde, and then we went straite thro' the House, into the Garden behind, which is on a rising Ground, with pleached Alleys and turfen Walks, and a Peep of the Church through the Trees. A Lad tolde us his Mistress was with the Bees, soe we walked towards the Hives; and, from an Arbour hard by, hearde a Murmur, though not of Bees, issuing. In this rusticall Bowre, found *Roger Agnew* reading to *Rose* and to Mr. *Milton*. Thereupon ensued manie cheerfulle Salutations, and *Rose* proposed returning to the House, but Master *Agnew* sayd it was pleasanter in the Bowre, where was Room for alle; soe then *Rose* offered to take me to her Chamber to lay aside my Hoode, and promised to send a Junkett into the Arbour; whereon Mr. *Agnew* smiled at Mr. *Milton*, and sayd somewhat of "neat-handed "*Phillis.*"

As we went alonge, I tolde *Rose* I had seene her Guest once before, and thought him

him a comely, pleasant Gentleman. She laught, and sayd, " Pleasant? why, he is " one of the greatest Scholars of our Time, " and knows more Languages than you " or I ever hearde of." I made Answer, " That may be, and yet might not ensure " his being pleasant, but rather the con- " trary, for I cannot reade *Greeke* and *Latin*, " *Rose*, like you." Quoth *Rose*, " But " you can reade *English*, and he hath writ " some of the loveliest *English* Verses " you ever hearde, and hath brought " us a new Composure this Morning, " which *Roger*, being his olde College " Friend, was discussing with him, to my " greate Pleasure, when you came. After " we have eaten the Junkett, he shall " beginne it again." " By no Means," said I, " for I love Talking more than " Reading." However, it was not soe to be, for *Rose* woulde not be foyled; and as it woulde not have been good Manners to decline the Hearinge in Presence of the Poet, I was constrayned to suppresse a secret Yawne, and feign Attention, though,
Truth

Truth to say, it soone wandered; and, during the laste halfe Hour, I sat in a compleat Dreame, tho' not unpleasant one. *Roger* having made an End, 'twas diverting to heare him commending the Piece unto the Author, who as gravely accepted it; yet, with nothing fullesome about the one, or misproud about the other. Indeed, there was a sedate Sweetnesse in the Poet's Wordes as well as Lookes; and shortlie, waiving the Discussion of his owne Composures, he beganne to talke of those of other Men, as *Shakspeare*, *Spenser*, *Cowley*, *Ben Jonson*, and of *Tasso*, and *Tasso's* Friend the Marquis of *Villa*, whome, it appeared, Mr. *Milton* had Knowledge of in *Italy*. Then he askt me, woulde I not willingly have seene the Country of *Romeo* and *Juliet*, and prest to know whether I loved Poetry; but finding me loath to tell, sayd he doubted not I preferred Romances, and that he had read manie, and loved them dearly too. I sayd, I loved *Shakspeare's* Plays better than *Sidney's* Arcadia; on which he cried "Righte," and drew nearer
to

to me, and woulde have talked at greater length; but, knowing from *Rose* how learned he was, I feared to shew him I was a sillie Foole; soe, like a sillie Foole, held my Tongue.

Dinner; Eggs, Bacon, roast Ribs of Lamb, Spinach, Potatoes, savoury Pie, a *Brentford* Pudding, and Cheesecakes. What a pretty Housewife *Rose* is! *Roger's* plain Hospitalitie and scholarlie Discourse appeared to much Advantage. He askt of News from *Paris;* and Mr. *Milton* spoke much of the *Swedish* Ambassadour, *Dutch* by Birth; a Man renowned for his Learning, Magnanimity, and Misfortunes, of whome he had seene much. He tolde *Rose* and me how this Mister *Van der Groote* had beene unjustlie caste into Prison by his Countrymen; and how his good Wife had shared his Captivitie, and had tried to get his Sentence reversed; failing which, she contrived his Escape in a big Chest, which she pretended to be full of heavie olde Bookes. Mr. *Milton* concluded with the Exclamation, "Indeede, there never

"was

"was such a Woman;" on which, deare *Roger*, whome I beginne to love, quoth, "Oh yes, there are manie such,—we have "two at Table now." Whereat, Mr. *Milton* smiled.

At Leave-taking pressed Mr. *Agnew* and *Rose* to come and see us soone; and *Dick* askt Mr. *Milton* to see the Bowling Greene.

Ride Home, delightfulle.

May 14*th*.

THOUGHT, when I woke this Morning, I had been dreaminge of *St. Paul* let down the Wall in a Basket; but founde, on more closely examining the Matter, 'twas *Grotius* carried down the Ladder in a Chest; and methought I was his Wife, leaninge from the Window above, and crying to the Souldiers, "Have a Care, "have a Care!" 'Tis certayn I shoulde have betraied him by an Over-anxietie.

Resolved to give *Father* a *Sheepscote* Dinner,

Dinner, but *Margery* affirmed the Haunch woulde no longer keepe, so was forced to have it drest, though meaninge to have kept it for Companie. Little *Kate*, who had been out alle the Morning, came in with her Lap full of Butter-burs, the which I was glad to see, as *Mother* esteemes them a sovereign Remedie 'gainst the Plague, which is like to be rife in *Oxford* this Summer, the Citie being so overcrowded on account of his Majestie. While laying them out on the Stille-room Floor, in bursts *Robin* to say Mr. *Agnew* and Mr. *Milton* were with *Father* at the Bowling Greene, and woulde dine here. So was glad *Margery* had put down the Haunch. 'Twas past one o' the Clock, however, before it coulde be sett on Table; and I had just run up to pin on my Carnation Knots, when I hearde them alle come in discoursing merrilie.

At Dinner Mr. *Milton* askt *Robin* of his Studdies; and I was in Payne for the deare Boy, knowing him to be better affected to his out-doore Recreations than to to his Booke; but he answered boldlie he was in *Ovid*, and I lookt in Mr. *Milton's* Face to guesse was that goode Scholarship or no; but he turned it towards my *Father*, and sayd he was trying an Experiment on two young Nephews of his owne, whether the reading those Authors that treate of physical Subjects mighte not advantage them more than the Poets; whereat my *Father* jested with him, he being himselfe one of the Fraternitie he seemed to despise. But he uphelde his Argumente so bravelie, that *Father* listened in earneste Silence. Meantime, the Cloth being drawne, and I in Feare of remaining over long, was avised to withdrawe myselfe earlie, *Robin* following, and begging me to goe downe to the Fish-ponds. Afterwards alle the others joyned us, and we sate on the Steps till the Sun went down, when, the Horses being broughte round, our Guests tooke Leave without returning to the House. *Father* walked thoughtfullie Home with me, leaning on my Shoulder, and spake little.

May

May 15*th.*

AFTER writing the above last Night, in my Chamber, went to Bed and had a most heavenlie Dreame. Methoughte it was brighte, brighte Moonlighte, and I was walking with Mr. *Milton* on a Terrace,—not *our* Terrace, but in some outlandish Place; and it had Flights and Flights of green Marble Steps, descending, I cannot tell how farre, with Stone Figures and Vases on everie one. We went downe and downe these Steps, till we came to a faire Piece of Water, still in the Moonlighte; and then, methoughte, he woulde be taking Leave, and sayd much aboute Absence and Sorrowe, as tho' we had knowne eache other some Space; and alle that he sayd was delightfulle to heare. Of a suddain we hearde Cries, as of Distresse, in a Wood that came quite down to the Water's Edge, and Mr. *Milton* sayd, "Hearken!" and then, "There is some "one being slaine in the Woode, I must "goe

"goe to rescue him;" and soe, drewe his Sword and ran off. Meanwhile, the Cries continued, but I did not seeme to mind them much; and, looking stedfastlie downe into the cleare Water, coulde see to an immeasurable Depth, and beheld, oh, rare! Girls sitting on glistening Rocks, far downe beneathe, combing and braiding their brighte Hair, and talking and laughing, onlie I coulde not heare aboute what. And theire Kirtles were like spun Glass, and theire Bracelets Coral and Pearl; and I thought it the fairest Sight that Eyes coulde see. But, alle at once, the Cries in the Wood affrighted them, for they started, looked upwards and alle aboute, and began swimming thro' the cleare Water so fast, that it became troubled and thick, and I coulde see them noe more. Then I was aware that the Voices in the Wood were of *Dick* and *Harry*, calling for *me*; and I soughte to answer, "Here!" but my Tongue was heavie. Then I commenced running towards them, through ever so manie greene Paths, in the Wood;

but

but still, we coulde never meet; and I began to see grinning Faces, neither of Man nor Beaste, peeping at me through the Trees; and one and another of them called me by Name; and in greate Feare and Paine I awoke!

. . . Strange Things are Dreames. Dear *Mother* thinks much of them, and sayth they oft portend coming Events. My *Father* holdeth the Opinion that they are rather made up of what hath alreadie come to passe; but surelie naught like this Dreame of mine hath in anie Part befallen me hithertoe?

. . . What strange Fable or Masque were they reading that Day at *Sheepscote?* I mind not.

May 20*th.*

TOO much busied of late to write, though much hath happened which I woulde fain remember. Dined at *Shotover* yesterday. Met *Mother*, who is coming Home in a Day or two, but helde short Speech

Speech with me aside concerning House-wifery. The *Agnews* there, of course: alsoe Mr. *Milton*, whom we have seene continuallie, lately; and I know not how it shoulde be, but he seemeth to like me. *Father* affects him much, but *Mother* loveth him not. She hath seene little of him: perhaps the less the better. *Ralph Hewlett*, as usuall, forward in his rough Endeavours to please; but, though no Scholar, I have yet Sense enough to prefer Mr. *Milton's* Discourse to his. . . . I wish I were fonder of Studdy; but, since it cannot be, what need to vex? Some are born of one Mind, some of another. *Rose* was al-waies for her Booke; and, had *Rose* beene no Scholar, Mr. *Agnew* woulde, may be, never have given her a second Thoughte: but alle are not of the same Way of thinking.

. . . A few Lines received from *Mother's* "spoilt Boy," as *Father* hath called Brother *Bill*, ever since he went a soldiering. Blurred and mis-spelt as they are, she will prize them. Trulie, we are none of us
grate

grate hands at the Pen; 'tis well I make this my Copie-booke.

... Oh, strange Event! Can this be Happinesse? Why, then, am I soe feared, soe mazed, so prone to weeping? I woulde that *Mother* were here. Lord have Mercie on me a sinfulle, sillie Girl, and guide my Steps arighte.

... It seemes like a Dreame, (I have done noughte but dreame of late, I think,) my going along the matted Passage, and hearing Voices in my *Father's* Chamber, just as my Hand was on the Latch; and my withdrawing my Hand, and going softlie away, though I never paused at disturbing him before; and, after I had beene a full Houre in the stille Room, turning over ever soe manie Trays full of dried Herbs and Flower-leaves, hearing him come forthe and call, " *Moll*, deare " *Moll*, where are you?" with I know not what of strange in the Tone of his Voice; and my running to him hastilie, and his drawing me into his Chamber, and closing the Doore. Then he takes
me

me round the Waiste, and remains quite silent awhile; I gazing on him so strangelie! and at length, he says with a Kind of Sigh, "Thou art indeed but young "yet! scarce seventeen,—and fresh, as "Mr. *Milton* says, as the earlie May; too "tender, forsooth, to leave us yet, sweet "Child! But what wilt say, *Moll*, when "I tell thee that a well-esteemed Gentle-"man, whom as yet indeed I know too "little of, hath craved of me Access to the "House as one that woulde win your "Favour?"

Thereupon, such a suddain Faintness of the Spiritts overtooke me, (a Thing I am noe way subject to,) as that I fell down in a Swound at *Father's* Feet; and when I came to myselfe agayn, my Hands and Feet seemed full of Prickles, and there was a Humming, as of *Rose's* Bees, in mine Ears. *Lettice* and *Margery* were tending of me, and *Father* watching me full of Care; but soe soone as he saw me open mine Eyes, he bade the Maids stand aside, and sayd, stooping over me, "Enough,

"Enough, dear *Moll;* we will talk noe more of this at present." "Onlie just tell me," quoth I, in a Whisper, "who it is." "Guesse," sayd he. "I cannot," I softlie replied; and, with the Lie, came such a Rush of Blood to my Cheeks as betraied me. "I am sure you have though," said deare *Father*, gravelie, "and I neede not say it is Mr. *Milton*, of whome I know little more than you doe, and that is not enough. On the other hand, *Roger Agnew* sayth that he is one of whome we can never know too much, and there is somewhat about him which inclines me to believe it." "What will *Mother* say?" interrupted I. Thereat *Father's* Countenance changed; and he hastilie answered, "Whatever she likes: I have an Answer for her, and a Question too;" and abruptlie left me, bidding me keepe myselfe quiet.

But can I? Oh, no! *Father* hath sett a Stone rolling, unwitting of its Course. It hath prostrated me in the first Instance, and will, I misdoubt, hurt my *Mother*. *Father*

Father is bold enow in her Absence, but when she comes back will leave me to face her Anger alone; or else, make such a Stir to shew that he is not governed by a Woman, as wille make Things worse. Meanwhile, how woulde I have them? Am I most pleased or payned? dismayed or flattered? Indeed, I know not.

. . . I am soe sorry to have swooned. Needed I have done it, merelie to heare there was one who soughte my Favour? Aye, but one so wise! so thoughtfulle! so unlike me!

Bedtime; same Daye.

. . . . . .

WHO knoweth what a Daye will bring forth? After writing the above, I sate like one stupid, ruminating on I know not what, except on the Unlikelihood that one soe wise woulde trouble himselfe to *seeke* for aught and yet fail to *win*. After abiding a long Space in mine owne Chamber,

Chamber, alle below seeming still, I began to wonder shoulde we dine alone or not, and to have a hundred hot and cold Fitts of Hope and Feare. Thought I, if Mr. *Milton* comes, assuredlie I cannot goe down; but yet I must; but yet I will not; but yet the best will be to conduct myselfe as though nothing had happened; and, as he seems to have left the House long ago, maybe he hath returned to *Sheepscote*, or even to *London*. Oh that *London!* Shall I indeede ever see it? and the rare Shops, and the Play-houses, and *St. Paul's*, and the *Towre?* But what and if that ever comes to pass? Must I leave Home? dear *Forest Hill?* and *Father* and *Mother*, and the Boys? more especiallie *Robin?* Ah! but *Father* will give me a long Time to think of it. He will, and must.

Then Dinner-time came; and, with Dinner-time, Uncle *Hewlett* and *Ralph*, Squire *Paice* and Mr. *Milton*. We had a huge Sirloin, soe no Feare of short Commons. I was not ill pleased to see soe manie:

manie: it gave me an Excuse for holding my Peace, but I coulde have wished for another Woman. However, *Father* never thinks of that, and *Mother* will soone be Home. After Dinner the elder Men went to the Bowling-greene with *Dick* and *Ralph*; the Boys to the Fish-ponds; and, or ever I was aware, Mr. *Milton* was walking with me on the Terrace. My Dreame came soe forcibly to Mind, that my Heart seemed to leap into my Mouth; but he kept away from the Fish-ponds, and from Leave-taking, and from his morning Discourse with my *Father*,—at least for awhile; but some Way he got round to it, and sayd soe much, and soe well, that, after alle my *Father's* bidding me keepe quiete and take my Time, and mine owne Resolution to think much and long, he never rested till he had changed the whole Appearance of Things, and made me promise to be his, wholly and trulie.— And oh! I feare I have been too quickly wonne!

May

The Bowling Green at Forest Hill

May 23rd.

AT leaste, so sayeth the Calendar; but with me it hath beene trulie an *April* Daye, alle Smiles and Teares. And now my Spiritts are soe perturbed and dismaid, as that I know not whether to weepe or no, for methinks crying would relieve me. At first waking this Morning my Mind was elated at the Falsitie of my *Mother's* Notion, that no Man of Sense woulde think me worth the having; and soe I got up too proude, I think, and came down too vain, for I had spent an unusuall Time at the Glasse. My Spiritts, alsoe, were soe unequall, that the Boys took Notice of it, and it seemed as though I coulde breathe nowhere but out of Doors; so the Children and I had a rare Game of Play in the Home-close; but ever and anon I kept looking towards the Road and listening for Horses' Feet, till *Robin* sayd, "One would think the King was
"coming:"

"coming:" but at last came Mr. *Milton*, quite another Way, walking through the Fields with huge Strides. *Kate* saw him firste, and tolde me; and then sayd, "What makes you look soe pale?"

. . . . . .

We sate a good Space under the Hawthorn Hedge on the Brow of the Hill, listening to the Mower's Scythe, and the Song of Birds, which seemed enough for him, without talking; and as he spake not, I helde my Peace, till, with the Sun in my Eyes, I was like to drop asleep; which, as his own Face was *from* me, and towards the Landskip, he noted not. I was just aiming, for Mirthe's Sake, to steale away, when he suddainlie turned about and fell to speaking of rurall Life, Happinesse, Heaven, and such like, in a Kind of Rapture; then, with his Elbow half raising him from the Grass, lay looking at me; then commenced humming or singing I know not what Strayn, but 'twas of "*begli Occhi*" and "*Chioma aurata;*" and he kept smiling the while he sang.

After

After a time we went In-doors; and then came my firste Pang: for *Father* founde out how I had pledged myselfe overnighte; and for a Moment looked soe grave, that my Heart misgave me for having beene soe hastie. However, it soone passed off; deare *Father's* Countenance cleared, and he even seemed merrie at Table; and soon after Dinner alle the Party dispersed save Mr. *Milton*, who loitered with me on the Terrace. After a short Silence he exclaimed, "How good " is our God to us in alle his Gifts! For " Instance, in this Gift of *Love*, whereby " had he withdrawn from visible Nature a " thousand of its glorious Features and gay " Colourings, we shoulde stille possess, "*from within*, the Means of throwing over " her clouded Face an entirelie different " Hue! while as it is, what was pleasing " before now pleaseth more than ever! " Is it not soe, sweet *Moll?* May I express " thy Feelings as well as mine own, un- " blamed? or am I too adventurous? You " are silent; well, then, let me believe
"that

"that we think alike, and that the Emo-
"tions of the few laste Hours have given
"such an Impulse to alle that is high, and
"sweete, and deepe, and pure, and holy in
"our innermoste Hearts, as that we seeme
"now onlie firste to taste the *Life of Life*,
"and to perceive how much nearer Earth
"is to Heaven than we thought! Is it
"soe? Is it not soe?" and I was constrayned to say "Yes," at I scarcelie knew
what; grudginglie too, for I feared having
once alreadie sayd "Yes" too soone. But
he saw nought amisse, for he was expecting nought amisse; soe went on, most like
Truth and Love that Lookes could speake
or Wordes sounde: "Oh, I know it, I
"feel it:—henceforthe there is a Life re-
"served for us in which Angels may sym-
"pathize. For this most excellent Gift
"of Love shall enable us to read together
"the whole Booke of Sanctity and Virtue,
"and emulate eache other in carrying
"it into Practice; and as the wise *Magians*
"kept theire Eyes steadfastlie fixed on the
"Star, and followed it righte on, through
"rough

"Mr Milton loitered with me on the Terrace"

" rough and smoothe, soe we, with this
" bright Beacon, which indeed is set on
" Fire of Heaven, shall pass on through
" the peacefull Studdies, surmounted Ad-
" versities, and victorious Agonies of Life,
" ever looking steadfastlie up ! "

Alle this, and much more, as tedious to heare as to write, did I listen to, firste with flagging Attention, next with concealed Wearinesse ;—and as Wearinesse, if indulged, never *is* long concealed, it soe chanced, by Ill-luck, that Mr. *Milton*, suddainlie turning his Eyes from Heaven upon poor me, caughte, I can scarcelie expresse how slighte, an Indication of Discomforte in my Face ; and instantlie a Cloud crossed his owne, though as thin as that through which the Sun shines while it floats over him. Oh, 'twas not of a Moment ! and yet *in that Moment* we seemed eache to have seene the other, though but at a Glance, under new Circumstances :—as though two Persons at a Masquerade had just removed their Masques and put them on agayn. This gave me my seconde Pang :—

Pang:—I felt I had given him Payn; and though he made as though he forgot it directly, and I tooke Payns to make him forget it, I coulde never be quite sure whether he had.

. . . My Spiritts were soe dashed by this, and by learning his Age to be soe much more than I had deemed it, (for he is thirty-five! who coulde have thoughte it?) that I had, thenceforthe, the Aire of being much more discreete and pensive than belongeth to my Nature; whereby he was, perhaps, well pleased. As I became more grave he became more gay; soe that we met eache other, as it were, Half-way, and became righte pleasant. If his Countenance were comely before, it is quite heavenlie now; and yet I question whether my Love increaseth as rapidlie as my Feare. Surelie my Folly will prove as distastefull to him, as his over-much Wisdom to me. The Dread of it hath alarmed me alreadie. What has become, even now, of alle my gay Visions of Marriage, and *London*, and the Play-houses, and

and the *Towre?* They have faded away thus earlie, and in their Place comes a Foreboding of I can scarce say what. I am as if a Child, receiving from some olde Fairy the Gift of what seemed a fayre Doll's House, shoulde hastilie open the Doore thereof, and starte back at beholding nought within but a huge Cavern, deepe, high, and vaste; in parte glittering with glorious Chrystals, and the Rest hidden in obscure Darknesse.

May 24*th.*

DEAR *Rose* came this Morning. I flew forthe to welcome her, and as I drew near, she lookt upon me with such a Kind of Awe as that I could not forbeare laughing. Mr. *Milton* having slept at *Sheepscote,* had made her privy to our Engagement; for indeede, he and Mr. *Agnew* are such Friends, he will keep nothing from him. Thus *Rose* heares it before

before my owne Mother, which shoulde not be. When we had entered my Chamber, she embraced me once and agayn, and seemed to think soe much of my uncommon Fortune, that I beganne to think more of it myselfe. To heare her talke of Mr. *Milton* one would have supposed her more in Love with him than I. Like a Bookworm as she is, she fell to praysing his Composures. "Oh, "the leaste I care for in him is his "Versing," quoth I; and from that Moment a Spiritt of Mischief tooke Possession of me, to do a thousand heedlesse, ridiculous Things throughoute the Day, to shew *Rose* how little I set by the Opinion of soe wise a Man. Once or twice Mr. *Milton* lookt earnestlie and questioninglie at me, but I heeded him not.

. . . Discourse at Table graver and less pleasant, methoughte, than heretofore. Mr. *Busire* having dropt in, was avised to ask Mr. *Milton* why, having had an university Education, he had not entered

entered the Church. He replied, drylie enough, because he woulde not subscribe himselfe *Slave* to anie Formularies of Men's making. I saw *Father* bite his Lip; and *Roger Agnew* mildly observed, he thought him wrong; for that it was not for an Individual to make Rules for another Individual, but yet that the generall Voice of the Wise and Good, removed from the pettie Prejudices of private Feeling, mighte pronounce authoritativelie wherein an Individual was righte or wrong, and frame Laws to keepe him in the righte Path. Mr. *Milton* replyed, that manie Fallibles could no more make up an Infallible than manie Finites could make an Infinite. Mr. *Agnew* rejoyned, that ne'erthelesse, an Individual who opposed himselfe agaynst the generall Current of the Wise and Good, was, leaste of alle, likelie to be in the Right; and that the Limitations of human Intellect which made the Judgment of manie wise Men liable to Question, certainlie made the Judgment of *anie* wise Man, self-

self-dependent, more questionable still. Mr. *Milton* shortlie replied that there were Particulars in the required Oaths which made him unable to take them without Perjurie. And soe, an End: but 'twas worth a World to see *Rose* looking soe anxiouslie from the one Speaker to the other, desirous that eache should be victorious; and I was sorry that it lasted not a little longer.

As *Rose* and I tooke our Way to the Summer-house, she put her Arm round me, saying, "How charming is divine "Philosophie!" I coulde not helpe asking if she did not meane how charming was the Philosophie of one particular Divine? Soe then she discoursed with me of Things more seemlie for Women than Philosophie or Divinitie either. Onlie, when Mr. *Agnew* and Mr. *Milton* joyned us, she woulde aske them to repeat one Piece of Poetry after another, beginning with *Carew's*—

"*He who loves a rosie Cheeke,
Or a coral Lip admires,—*"

And

And crying at the End of eache, " Is not "that lovely? Is not that divine?" I franklie sayd I liked none of them soe much as some Mr. *Agnew* had recited, concluding with—

> "*Mortals that would follow me,
> Love Virtue: she alone is free.*"

Whereon Mr. *Milton* surprised me with a suddain Kiss, to the immoderate Mirthe of *Rose*, who sayd I coulde not have looked more discomposed had he pretended he was the Author of those Verses. I afterwards found he *was*; but I think she laught more than there was neede.

We have ever been considered a sufficientlie religious Familie: that is, we goe regularly to Church on Sabbaths and Prayer-dayes, and keepe alle the Fasts and Festivalles. But Mr. *Milton's* Devotion hath attayned a Pitch I can neither imitate nor even comprehende. The spirituall World seemeth to him not onlie reall, but I may almoste say visible. For instance, he tolde *Rose*, it appears, that on
Tuesday

Tuesday Nighte, (that is the same Evening I had promised to be his,) as he went homewards to his Farm-lodging, he fancied the Angels whisperinge in his Eares, and singing over his Head, and that instead of going to his Bed like a reasonable Being, he lay down on the Grass, and gazed on the sweete, pale Moon till she sett, and then on the bright Starres till he seemed to see them moving in a slowe, solemn Dance, to the Words, " *How glorious is our God!*" And alle about him, he said, he *knew*, tho' he coulde not see them, were spirituall Beings repairing the Ravages of the Day on the Flowers, amonge the Trees, and Grasse, and Hedges; and he believed 'twas onlie the Filme that originall Sin had spread over his Eyes, that prevented his seeing them. I am thankful for this same Filme,—I cannot abide Fairies, and Witches, and Ghosts—ugh! I shudder even to write of them; and were it onlie of the more harmlesse Sort, one woulde never have the Comforte of thinkinge to be

be alone. I feare Churchyardes and dark Corners of alle Kinds; more especiallie Spiritts; and there is onlie one I would even wish to see at my bravest, when deepe Love casteth out Feare; and that is of Sister *Anne*, whome I never associate with the Worme and Winding-sheete. Oh no! I think *she*, at leaste, dwells amonge the Starres, having sprung straite up into Lighte and Blisse the Moment she put off Mortalitie; and if she, why not others? Are *Adam* and *Abraham* alle these Yeares in the unconscious Tomb? Theire Bodies, but surelie not their Spiritts? else, why dothe *Christ* speak of *Lazarus* lying in *Abraham's* Bosom, while the Brothers of *Dives* are yet riotouslie living? Yet what becomes of the Daye of generall Judgment, if some be thus pre-judged? I must aske Mr. *Milton*,—yes, I thinke I can finde it in my Heart to aske him about this in some solemn, stille Hour, and perhaps he will sett at Rest manie Doubts and Misgivings that at sundrie Times trouble me; being soe wise a Man.
Bedtime.

Bedtime.

. . . . .

LAD to steale away from the noisie Companie in the Supper-roome, (comprising some of *Father's* Fellow-magistrates,) I went down with *Robin* and *Kate* to the Fish-ponds; it was scarce Sunset: and there, while we threw Crumbs to the Fish and watched them come to the Surface, were followed, or ever we were aware, by Mr. *Milton,* who sate down on the stone Seat, drew *Robin* between his Knees, stroked his Haire, and askt what we were talking about. *Robin* sayd I had beene telling them a fairie Story; and Mr. *Milton* observed that was an infinite Improvement on the jangling, puzzle-headed Prating of Country Justices, and wished I woulde tell it agayn. But I was afrayd. But *Robin* had no Feares; soe tolde the Tale roundlie; onlie he forgot the End. Soe he found his Way backe to the Middle, and seemed likelie

to

"I went down with John and Kate to the Fish-Pond."

to make it last alle Night; onlie Mr.
Milton sayd he seemed to have got into
the Labyrinth of *Crete*, and he must for
Pitie's Sake give him the Clew. Soe
he finished *Robin's* Story, and then tolde
another, a most lovelie one, of Ladies,
and Princes, and Enchanters, and a brazen
Horse, and he sayd the End of *that* Tale
had been cut off too, by Reason the
Writer had died before he finished it.
But *Robin* cryed, "Oh! finish this too,"
and hugged and kist him; soe he did;
and methoughte the End was better than
the Beginninge. Then he sayd, "Now,
" sweet *Moll*, you have onlie spoken this
" Hour past, by your Eyes; and we
" must heare your pleasant Voice." "An
" Hour?" cries *Robin*. "Where are alle
" the red Clouds gone, then?" quoth
Mr. *Milton*, " and what Business hathe
" the Moon yonder?" "Then we must
" go Indoors," quoth I. But they cried
" No," and *Robin* helde me fast, and Mr.
Milton sayd I might know even by the
distant Sounds of ill-governed Merriment
that

that we were winding up the Week's Accounts of Joy and Care more consistentlie where we were than we coulde doe in the House. And indeede just then I hearde my *Father's* Voice swelling a noisie Chorus; and hoping Mr. *Milton* did not distinguish it, I askt him if he loved Musick. He answered, soe much that it was Miserie for him to hear anie that was not of the beste. I secretlie resolved he should never heare mine. He added, he was come of a musicalle Familie, and that his Father not onlie sang well, but played finely on the Viol and Organ. Then he spake of the sweet Musick in *Italy*, untill I longed to be there; but I tolde him nothing in its Way ever pleased me more than to heare the Choristers of *Magdalen* College usher in *May* Day by chaunting a Hymn at the Top of the Church Towre. Discoursing of this and that, we thus sate a good While ere we returned to the House.

. . . Coming out of Church he woulde shun

shun the common Field, where the Villagery led up theire Sports, saying, he deemed Quoit-playing and the like to be unsuitable Recreations on a Daye whereupon the *Lord* had restricted us from speakinge our own Words, and thinking our own (that is, secular) Thoughts: and that he believed the Law of *God* in this Particular woulde soone be the Law of the Land, for Parliament woulde shortlie put down *Sunday* Sports. I askt, "What, "the *King's* Parliament at *Oxford?*" He answered, "No; *the Country's* Parliament "at *Westminster.*" I sayd, I was sorrie, for manie poore hard-working Men had no other Holiday. He sayd, another Holiday woulde be given them; and that whether or no, we must not connive at Evil, which we doe in permitting an *holy Daye* to sink into a Holiday. I sayd, but was it not the *Jewish* Law, which had made such Restrictions? He sayd, yes, but that *Christ* came not to destroy the moral Law, of which Sabbath-keeping was a Part, and that even its naturall
Fitnesse

Fitnesse for the bodily Welfare of Man and Beast was such as no wise Legislator would abolish or abuse it, even had he no Consideration for our spiritual and immortal Part: and that 'twas a well-known Fact that Beasts of Burthen, which had not one Daye of Rest in seven, did lesse Worke in the End. As for oure Soules, he sayd, they required theire spiritual Meales as much as our Bodies required theires; and even poore, rusticall Clownes who coulde not reade, mighte nourish their better Parts by an holie Pause, and by looking within them, and around them, and above them. I felt inclined to tell him that long Sermons alwaies seemed to make me love *God* less insteade of more, but woulde not, fearing he mighte take it that I meant *he* had been giving me one.

Monday.

Monday.

MOTHER hath returned! The Moment I hearde her Voice I fell to trembling. At the same Moment I hearde *Robin* cry, "Oh, "*Mother*, I have broken "the greene Beaker!" which betraied Apprehension in another Quarter. However, she quite mildlie replied, "Ah, I "knew the Handle was loose," and then kist me with soe great Affection that I felt quite easie. She had beene withhelde by a troublesome Colde from returning at the appointed Time, and cared not to write. 'Twas just Supper-time, and there were the Children to kiss and to give theire Bread and Milk, and *Bill's* Letter to reade; soe that nothing particular was sayd till the younger Ones were gone to Bed, and *Father* and *Mother* were taking some Wine and Toast. Then says *Father*, "Well, Wife, have you got "the five hundred Pounds?" "No," she answers, rather carelesslie. "I tolde "you

"you how 'twould be," says *Father*; "you mighte as well have stayed at "Home." "Really, Mr. *Powell*," says *Mother*, "soe seldom as I stir from my "owne Chimney-corner, you neede not "to grudge me, I think, a few Dayes "among our mutuall Relatives." "I "shall goe to Gaol," says *Father*. "Non- "sense," says *Mother*; "to Gaol indeed!" "Well, then, who is to keepe me from "it?" says *Father*, laughing. "I will "answer for it, Mr. *Milton* will wait a "little longer for his Money," says *Mother*, "he is an honourable Man, I "suppose." "I wish he may thinke me "one," says *Father*; "and as to a little "longer, what is the goode of waiting for "what is as unlikelie to come eventuallie "as now?" "You must answer that for "yourselfe," says *Mother*, looking wearie: "I have done what I can, and can doe no "more." "Well, then, 'tis lucky Matters "stand as they do," says *Father*. "Mr. "*Milton* has been much here in your "Absence, my Dear, and has taken a
"Liking

"Liking to our *Moll;* soe, believing him, "as you say, to be an honourable Man, "I have promised he shall have her." "Nonsense," cries *Mother*, turning red and then pale. "Never farther from "Nonsense," says *Father*, "for 'tis to be, "and by the Ende of the Month too." "You are bantering me, Mr. *Powell*," says *Mother*. "How can you suppose "soe, my Deare?" says *Father*, "you doe "me Injustice." "Why, *Moll!*" cries *Mother*, turning sharplie towards me, as I sate mute and fearfulle, "what is alle "this, Child? You cannot, you dare "not think of wedding this round-headed "Puritan." "Not round-headed," sayd I, trembling; "his Haire is as long and "curled as mine." "Don't bandy Words "with me, Girl," says *Mother* passionatelie, "see how unfit you are to have a House "of your owne, who cannot be left in "Charge of your *Father's* for a Fort- "nighte, without falling into Mischiefe!" "I won't have *Moll* chidden in that "Way," says *Father*, "she has fallen into
"noe

"noe Mischiefe, and has beene a dis-
"creete and dutifull Child." "Then it
"has beene alle your doing," says *Mother*,
"and you have forced the Child into this
"Match." "Noe Forcing whatever,"
says *Father*, "they like one another, and
"I am very glad of it, for it happens
"to be very convenient." "Convenient,
"indeed," repeats *Mother*, and falls a
weeping. Thereon I must needs weepe
too, but she says, "Begone to Bed; there
"is noe Neede that you shoulde sit
"by to heare your owne *Father* confesse
"what a Fool he has beene."

To my Bedroom I have come, but cannot yet seek my Bed; the more as I still
heare theire Voices in Contention below.

Tuesday.

THIS Morninge's Breakfaste was moste uncomfortable, I feeling like a checkt Child, scarce minding to looke up or to eat. *Mother*, with Eyes red and swollen, scarce speaking save to the Children; *Father*

Father directing his Discourse chieflie to *Dick*, concerning Farm Matters and the Rangership of *Shotover*, tho' 'twas easie to see his Mind was not with them. Soe soone as alle had dispersed to theire customed Taskes, and I was loitering at the Window, *Father* calls aloud to me from his Studdy. Thither I go, and find him and *Mother*, she sitting with her Back to both. "*Moll*," says *Father*, with great Determination, "you have accepted Mr. "*Milton* to please yourself, you will marry "him out of hand to please me." "Spare "me, spare me, Mr. *Powell*," interrupts *Mother*, "if the Engagement may not be "broken off, at the least precipitate it "not with this indecent haste. Post-"pone it till——" "Till when?" says *Father*. "Till the Child is olde enough "to know her owne Mind." "That is, "to put off an honourable Man on false "Pretences," says *Father*, "she is olde "enough to know it alreadie. Speake, "*Moll*, are you of your *Mother's* Mind to "give up Mr. *Milton* altogether?" I
                                                                                                                                         trembled,

trembled, but sayd, " No." " Then, as
" his Time is precious, and he knows
" not when he may leave his Home
" agayn, I save you the Trouble, Child,
" of naming a Day, for it shall be the
" *Monday* before *Whitsuntide*." Thereat
Mother gave a Kind of Groan; but as
for me, I had like to have fallen on the
Ground, for I had had noe Thought of
suche Haste. " See what you are doing,
" Mr. *Powell*," says *Mother*, compassionat-
ing me, and raising me up, though somewhat roughlie; " I prophecie Evil of this
" Match." " Prophets of Evil are sure to
" find Listeners," says *Father*, " but I am not
" one of them;" and soe left the Room.
Thereon my *Mother*, who alwaies feares him
when he has a Fit of Determination, loosed
the Bounds of her Passion, and chid me
so unkindlie, that, humbled and mortified,
I was glad to seeke my Chamber.

. . . Entering the Dining-room, however, I uttered a Shriek on seeing *Father*
fallen back in his Chair, as though in a
Fit, like unto that which terrified us a
Year

Year ago; and *Mother* hearing me call out, ran in, loosed his Collar, and soone broughte him to himselfe, tho' not without much Alarm to alle. He made light of it himselfe, and sayd 'twas merelie a suddain Rush of Blood to the Head, and woulde not be dissuaded from going out; but *Mother* was playnly smote at the Heart, and having lookt after him with some anxietie, exclaimed, " I shall neither " meddle nor make more in this Busi-" nesse: your *Father's* suddain Seizures " shall never be layd at my Doore;" and soe left me, till we met at Dinner. After the Cloth was drawne, enters Mr. *Milton*, who goes up to *Mother*, and with Gracefulnesse kisses her Hand; but she withdrewe it pettishly, and tooke up her Sewing, on the which he lookt at her wonderingly, and then at me; then at her agayne, as though he woulde reade her whole Character in her Face; which having seemed to doe, and to write the same in some private Page of his Heart, he never troubled her or himself with further

further Comment, but tooke up Matters just where he had left them last. Ere we parted we had some private Conference touching our Marriage, for hastening which he had soe much to say that I coulde not long contend with him, especiallie as I founde he had plainlie made out that *Mother* loved him not.

Wednesday.

HOUSE full of Companie, leaving noe Time to write nor think. *Mother* sayth, tho' she cannot forbode an happy Marriage, she will provide for a merrie Wedding, and hathe growne more than commonlie tender to me, and given me some Trinkets, a Piece of fine *Holland* Cloth, and enoughe of green Sattin for a Gown, that will stand on End with its owne Richnesse. She hathe me constantlie with her in the Kitchen, Pantrie, and Storeroom, telling me 'tis needfulle I shoulde improve

improve in Housewiferie, seeing I shall soe soone have a Home of my owne.

 But I think *Mother* knows not, and I am afeard to tell her, that Mr. *Milton* hath no House of his owne to carry me to, but onlie Lodgings, which have well suited his Bachelor State, but may not, 'tis likelie, beseeme a Lady to live in. He deems so himself, and sayeth we will look out for an hired House together, at our Leisure. Alle this he hath sayd to me in an Undertone, in *Mother's* Presence, she sewing at the Table and we sitting in the Window; and 'tis difficult to tell how much she hears, for she will aske no Questions, and make noe Comments, onlie compresses her Lips, which makes me think she knows.

 The Children are in turbulent Spiritts; but *Robin* hath done nought but mope and make Moan since he learnt he must soe soone lose me. A Thought hath struck me,—Mr. *Milton* educates his Sister's Sons; two Lads of about *Robin's* Age. What if he woulde consent to take my Brother under his Charge? perhaps *Father* would be willing.   *Saturday.*

Saturday.

LAST Visitt to *Sheepscote*,—at leaste, as *Mary Powell;* but kind *Rose* and *Roger Agnew* will give us the Use of it for a Week on our Marriage, and spend the Time with dear *Father* and *Mother*, who will neede their Kindnesse. *Rose* and I walked long aboute the Garden, her Arm round my Neck; and she was avised to say,

"*Cloth of Frieze, be not too bold,*
  Tho' thou be matcht with Cloth of Gold,—"

And then craved my Pardon for soe unmannerly a Rhyme, which indeede, methoughte, needed an Excuse, but exprest a Feare that I knew not (what she called) my high Destiny, and prayed me not to trifle with Mr. *Milton's* Feelings nor in his Sighte, as I had done the Daye she dined at *Forest Hill*. I laught, and sayd, he must take me as he found me: he was going to marry *Mary Powell*, not the *Wise Widow of Tekoah*. *Rose* lookt wistfullie, but

but I bade her take Heart, for I doubted not we shoulde content eache the other; and for the Rest, her Advice shoulde not be forgotten. Thereat, she was pacyfied.

May 22nd.

ALLE Bustle and Confusion, —slaying of Poultrie, making of Pastrie, etc. People coming and going, prest to dine and to sup, and refuse, and then stay, the colde Meats and Wines ever on the Table; and in the Evening, the Rebecks and Recorders sent for that we may dance in the Hall. My Spiritts have been most unequall; and this Evening I was overtaken with a suddain Faintnesse, such as I never but once before experienced. They would let me dance no more; and I was quite tired enoughe to be glad to sit aparte with Mr. *Milton* neare the Doore, with the Moon shining on us; untill at length he drew me out into the Garden. He spake of Happinesse and Home, and Hearts

Hearts knit in Love, and of heavenlie Espousals, and of Man being the Head of the Woman, and of our *Lord's* Marriage with the Church, and of white Robes, and the Bridegroom coming in Clouds of Glory, and of the Voices of singing Men and singing Women, and eternall Spring, and eternall Blisse, and much that I cannot call to Mind, and other-much that I coulde not comprehende, but which was in mine Ears as the Song of Birds, or Falling of Waters.

May 23rd.

ROSE hath come, and hath kindlie offered to help pack the Trunks, (which are to be sent off by the Waggon to *London,*) that I may have the more Time to devote to Mr. *Milton.* Nay, but he will soon have all my Time devoted to himself, and I would as lief spend what little remains in mine accustomed Haunts, after mine accustomed

accustomed Fashion. I had purposed a Ride on *Clover* this Morning, with *Robin*; but the poor Boy must I trow be disappointed.

——And for what? Oh me! I have hearde such a long Sermon on Marriage-duty and Service, that I am faine to sit down and weepe. But no, I must not, for they are waiting for me in the Hall, and the Guests are come and the Musick is tuning, and my Lookes must not betray me.—And now farewell, *Journall*; for *Rose*, who first bade me keepe you (little deeming after what Fashion), will now pack you up, and I will not close you with a heavie Strayn. *Robin* is calling me beneath the Window,—*Father* is sitting in the Shade, under the old Pear-tree, seemingly in gay Discourse with Mr. *Milton*. To-morrow the Village-bells will ring for the Marriage of

MARY POWELL.

———

London,

London,
Mr. Russell's, Taylor,
St. Bride's Churchyard.

OH Heaven! is this my new Home? my Heart sinkes alreadie. After the swete fresh Ayre of *Sheepscote*, and the Cleanliness, and the Quiet and the pleasant Smells, Sightes, and Soundes, alle whereof Mr. *Milton* enjoyed to the Full as keenlie as I, saying they minded him of *Paradise*,—how woulde *Rose* pitie me, could she view me in this close Chamber, the Floor whereof of dark, uneven Boards, must have beene layd, methinks, three hundred Years ago; the oaken Pannells, utterlie destitute of Polish and with sundrie Chinks; the Bed with dull brown Hangings, lined with as dull a greene, occupying Half the Space; and Half the Remainder being filled with dustie Books, whereof there are Store alsoe in every other Place. This Mirror,

I should thinke, belonged to faire *Rosamond*. And this Arm-chair to King *Lear*. Over the Chimnie hangs a ruefull Portrait,—maybe of *Grotius*, but I shoulde sooner deeme it of some Worthie before the Flood. Onlie one Quarter of the Casement will open, and that upon a Prospect, oh dolefulle! of the Churchyarde. Mr. *Milton* had need be as blythe as he was all the Time we were at *Sheepscote*, or I shall be buried in that same Churchyarde within the Twelvemonth. 'Tis well he has stepped out to see a Friend, that I may in his Absence get ridd of this Fit of the Dismalls. I wish it may be the last. What would *Mother* say to his bringing me to such a Home as this? I will not think. Soe this is *London*! How diverse from the " towred " Citie " of my Husband's versing! and of his Prose too; for as he spake, by the way, of the Disorders of our Time, which extend even into eache domestick Circle, he sayd that alle must, for a While, appear confused to our imperfect View, just as as a mightie Citie unto a Stranger who shoulde beholde around him huge, unfinished Fabrics, the Plan whereof he could but imperfectlie make out, amid the Builders' disorderlie Apparatus; but that, *from afar*, we mighte perceive glorious Results from party Contentions,—Freedom springing up from Opression, Intelligence succeeding Ignorance, Order following Disorder, just as that same Traveller looking at the Citie from a distant Height, should beholde Towres, and Spires glistering with Gold and Marble, Streets stretching in lessening Perspectives, and Bridges flinging their white Arches over noble Rivers. But what of this saw we all along the *Oxford* Road? Firstlie, there was noe commanding Height; second, there was the Citie obscured by a drizzling Rain; the Ways were foul, the Faces of those we mett spake less of Pleasure than Business, and Bells were tolling, but none ringing. Mr. *Milton's* Father, a grey-haired, kind old Man, was here to give us welcome: and

and his firste Words were, "Why, *John*, "thou hast stolen a March on us. Soe "quickly, too, and soe snug! But she "is faire enoughe, Man, to excuse thee, "Royalist or noe."

And soe, taking me in his Arms, kist me franklie.—But I heare my Husband's Voice, and another with it.

Thursday.

'T WAS a Mr. *Lawrence* whom my Husband brought Home last Nighte to sup; and the Evening passed righte pleasantlie, with News, Jestes, and a little Musicke. Todaye hath been kindlie devoted by Mr. *Milton* to shewing me Sights: and oh! the strange, diverting Cries in the Streets, even from earlie Dawn! "New Milk and Curds from "the Dairie!"—"Olde Shoes for some "Brooms!"—"Anie Kitchen-stuffe, have "you, Maids?"—"Come buy my greene "Herbes!"—and then in the Streets, here

here a Man preaching, there another juggling: here a Boy with an Ape, there a Show of *Nineveh:* next the News from the North; and as for the China Shops and Drapers in the *Strand,* and the Cook's Shops in *Westminster,* with the smoking Ribs of Beef and fresh Salads set out on Tables in the Street, and Men in white Aprons crying out, "Calf's Liver, Tripe, "and hot Sheep's Feet"—'twas enoughe to make One untimelie hungrie,—or take One's Appetite away, as the Case might be. Mr. *Milton* shewed me the noble Minster, with King *Harry* Seventh's Chapel adjoining; and pointed out the old House where *Ben Jonson* died. Neare the *Broade Sanctuarie,* we fell in with a slighte, dark-complexioned young Gentleman of two or three and twenty, whome my Husband espying cryed, "What, "*Marvell?*" the other comically answering, "What Marvel?" and then, handsomlie saluting me and complimenting Mr. *Milton,* much lighte and pleasant Discourse ensued; and finding we were aboute

"Strange doings (!) in the street"

aboute to take Boat, he volunteered to goe with us on the River. After manie Hours' Exercise, I have come Home fatigued, yet well pleased. Mr. *Marvell* sups with us.

Friday.

I WISH I could note down a Tithe of the pleasant Things that were sayd last Nighte. First, olde Mr. *Milton* having stept out with his Son,—I called in *Rachael*, the younger of Mr. *Russel's* Serving-maids, (for we have none of our owne as yet, which tends to much Discomfiture,) and, with her Aide, I dusted the Bookes and sett them up in half the Space they had occupied; then cleared away three large Basketfuls, of the absolutest Rubbish, torn Letters and the like, and sent out for Flowers, (which it seemeth strange enoughe to me to *buy*,) which gave the Chamber a gayer Aire, and soe my Husband sayd when he came in,

in, calling me the fayrest of them alle; and then, sitting down with Gayety to the Organ, drew forthe from it heavenlie Sounds. Afterwards Mr. *Marvell* came in, and they discoursed about *Italy*, and Mr. *Milton* promised his Friend some Letters of Introduction to *Jacopo Gaddi*, *Clementillo*, and others.

After Supper, they wrote Sentences, Definitions, and the like, after a Fashion of *Catherine de Medici*, some of which I have layd aside for *Rose*.

—To-day we have seene *St. Paul's* faire Cathedral, and the School where Mr. *Milton* was a Scholar when a Boy; thence, to the Fields of *Finsbury;* where are Trees and Windmills enow: a Place much frequented for practising Archery and other manlie Exercises.

Saturday.

Saturday.

HO' we rise betimes, olde Mr. *Milton* is earlier stille; and I always find him sitting at his Table beside the Window (by Reason of the Chamber being soe dark,) sorting I know not how manie Bundles of Papers tied with red Tape; eache so like the other that I marvel how he knows them aparte. This Morning, I found the poore old Gentleman in sad Distress at missing a Manuscript Song of Mr. *Henry Lawe's*, the onlie Copy extant, which he persuaded himselfe that I must have sent down to the Kitchen Fire Yesterday. I am convinced I dismist not a single Paper that was not torne eache Way, as being utterlie uselesse; but as the unluckie Song cannot be founde, he sighs and is certayn of my Delinquence, as is *Hubert*, his owne Man; or, as he more frequentlie calls him, his "odd "Man;"—and an odd Man indeede is
Mr.

Mr. *Hubert,* readie to address his Master or Master's Sonne on the merest Occasion, without waiting to be spoken to; tho' he expecteth Others to treat them with far more Deference than he himself payeth.

—Dead tired, this Daye, with so much Exercise; but woulde not say soe, because my Husband was thinking to please me by shewing me soe much. Spiritts flagging however. These *London* Streets wearie my Feet. We have been over the House in *Aldersgate Street,* the Garden whereof disappointed me, having hearde soe much of it; but 'tis far better than none, and the House is large enough for Mr. *Milton's* Familie and my *Father's* to boote. Thought how pleasant 'twould be to have them alle aboute me next *Christmasse;* but that holie Time is noe longer kept with Joyfulnesse in *London.* Ventured, therefore, to expresse a Hope, we mighte spend it at *Forest Hill;* but Mr. *Milton* sayd 'twas unlikelie he should be able to leave Home; and askt, would I go alone?—Constrained, for Shame, to say

say no; but felt, in my Heart, I woulde jump to see *Forest Hill* on anie Terms, I soe love alle that dwell there.

Sunday Even.

PRIVATE and publick Prayer, Sermons, and Psalm-singing from Morn until Nighte. The onlie Break hath been a Visit to a quaint but pleasing Quaker Lady, (the first of that Persuasion I have ever had Speech of,) by Name *Catherine Thompson,* whom my Husband holds in great Reverence. She said manie Things worthy to be remembered; onlie *as* I remember them, I need not to write them down. Sorrie to be caughte napping by my Husband, in the Midst of the third long Sermon. This comes of over-walking, and of being unable to sleep o' Nights; for whether it be the *London* Ayre, or the *London* Methods of making the Beds, or the strange Noises in in the Streets, I know not, but I have scarce beene able to close my Eyes before Daybreak since I came to Town.

Monday.

AND now beginneth a new Life; for my Husband's Pupils, who were dismist for a Time for my Sake, returne to theire Tasks this Daye, and olde Mr. *Milton* giveth Place to his two Grandsons, his widowed Daughter's Children, *Edward* and *John Philips*, whom my Husband led in to me just now. Two plainer Boys I never sett Eyes on; the one weak-eyed and puny, the other prim and puritanicall —no more to be compared to our sweet *Robin!* . . . After a few Words, they retired to theire Books; and my Husband, taking my Hand, sayd in his kindliest Manner,—" And now I leave my " sweete *Moll* to the pleasant Com- " panie of her own goode and innocent " Thoughtes; and, if she needs more, " here

"here are both stringed and keyed In-
"struments, and Books both of the older
"and modern Time, soe that she will not
"find the Hours hang heavie." Methoughte how much more I should like a
Ride upon *Clover* than all the Books that
ever were penned; for the Door no sooner
closed upon Mr. *Milton* than it seemed as
tho' he had taken alle the Sunshine with
him; and I fell to cleaning the Casement
that I mighte look out the better into the
Churchyarde, and then altered Tables and
Chairs, and then sate downe with my
Elbows resting on the Window-seat, and
my Chin on the Palms of my Hands,
gazing on I knew not what, and feeling
like a Butterflie under a Wine-glass.

 I marvelled why it seemed soe long
since I was married, and wondered what
they were doing at Home,—coulde fancy
I hearde *Mother* chiding, and see *Charlie*
stealing into the Dairie and dipping his
Finger in the Cream, and *Kate* feeding
the Chickens, and *Dick* taking a Stone
out of *Whitestar's* Shoe.

       —Methought

—Methought how dull it was to be passing the best Part of the Summer out of the Reache of fresh Ayre and greene Fields, and wondered, would alle my future Summers be soe spent?

Thoughte how dull it was to live in Lodgings, where one could not even go into the Kitchen to make a Pudding; and how dull to live in a Town, without some young female Friend with whom one might have ventured into the Streets, and where one could not soe much as feed Colts in a Paddock; how dull to be without a Garden, unable soe much as to gather a Handfulle of ripe Cherries; and how dull to looke into a Churchyarde, where there was a Man digging a Grave!

—When I wearied of staring at the Grave-digger, I gazed at an olde Gentleman and a young Lady slowlie walking along, yet scarce as if I noted them; and was thinking mostlie of *Forest Hill*, when I saw them stop at our Doore, and presently they were shewn in, by the Name of Doctor and Mistress *Davies*. I sent for my my Husband, and entertayned 'em bothe as well as I could, till he appeared, and they were polite and pleasant to me; the young Lady tall and slender, of a cleare brown Skin, and with Eyes that were fine enough; onlie there was a supprest Smile on her Lips alle the Time, as tho' she had seen me looking out of the Window. She tried me on all Subjects, I think; for she started them more adroitlie than I; and taking up a Book on the Window-seat, which was the *Amadigi* of *Bernardo Tasso*, printed alle in *Italiques*, she sayd, if I loved Poetry, which she was sure I must, she knew she shoulde love me. I did not tell her whether or noe. Then we were both silent. Then Doctor *Davies* talked vehementlie to Mr. *Milton* agaynst the King; and Mr. *Milton* was not so contrarie to him as I could have wished. Then Mistress *Davies* tooke the Word from her Father and beganne to talke to Mr. *Milton* of *Tasso*, and *Dante*, and *Boiardo*, and *Ariosto;* and then Doctor *Davies* and I were silent. Methoughte, they

they both talked well, tho' I knew so little
of their Subject-matter; onlie they com-
plimented eache other too much. I mean
not they were insincere, for eache seemed
to think highlie of the other; onlie we
neede not say alle we feele.

To conclude, we are to sup with them
to-morrow.

Wednesday.

JOURNALL, I have No-
bodie now but you, to
whome to tell my little
Griefs; indeede, before I
married, I know not that I
had anie; and even now,
they are very small, onlie they are soe new,
that sometimes my Heart is like to burst.

—I know not whether 'tis safe to put
them alle on Paper, onlie it relieves for
the Time, and it kills Time, and perhaps,
a little While hence I may looke back
and see how small they were, and how
they mighte have beene shunned, or better
borne. 'Tis worth the Triall.

—Yesterday

—Yesterday Morn, for very Wearinesse, I looked alle over my Linen and Mr. *Milton's*, to see could I finde anie Thing to mend; but there was not a Stitch amiss. I woulde have played on the Spinnette, but was afrayd he should hear my indifferent Musick. Then, as a last Resource, I tooke a Book—*Paul Perrin's Historie of the Waldenses;*—and was, I believe, dozing a little, when I was aware of a continuall Whispering and Crying. I thought 'twas some Child in the Street; and, having some Comfits in my Pocket, I stept softlie out to the House-door and lookt forth, but no Child could I see. Coming back, the Door of my Husband's Studdy being ajar, I was avised to look in; and saw him, with awfulle Brow, raising his Hand in the very Act to strike the youngest *Phillips*. I could never endure to see a Child struck, soe hastilie cryed out, "Oh, don't!"— whereon he rose, and, as if not seeing me, gently closed the Door, and, before I reached my Chamber, hearde soe loud a Crying that I began to cry too. Soon, alle

alle was quiet; and my Husband, coming in, stept gently up to me, and putting his Arm about my Neck, sayd, "My dearest "Life, never agayn, I beseech you, inter- "fere between me and the Boys: 'tis as "unseemlie as tho' I shoulde interfere be- "tween you and your Maids,—when you "have any,—and will weaken my Hands, "dear *Moll*, more than you have anie "suspicion of."

I replied, kissing that same offending Member as I spoke, "Poor *Jack* would "have beene glad, just now, if I *had* "weakened them."—"But that is not the "Question," he returned, "for we should "alle be glad to escape necessary Punish- "ment; whereas, it is the Power, not the "Penalty of our bad Habits, that we "shoulde seek to be delivered from."— "There may," I sayd, "be necessary, "but need not be corporal Punishment." "That is as may be," returned he, "and "hath alreadie been settled by an Autho- "ritie to which I submit, and partlie "think you will not dispute, and that is,
"the

"the Word of *God*. Pain of Body is in
"Realitie, or ought to be, sooner over and
"more safelie borne than Pain of an in-
"genuous Mind; and, as to the *Shame*,—
"why, as *Lorenzo de' Medici* sayd to *Soccini*,
"'The Shame is in the Offence rather
"than in the Punishment.'"

I replied, "Our *Robin* had never beene
"beaten for his Studdies;" to which he
sayd with a Smile, that even I must admit
Robin to be noe great Scholar. And so in
good Humour left me; but I was in no
good Humour, and hoped Heaven might
never make me the Mother of a Son, for
if I should see Mr. *Milton* strike him, I
should learn to hate the Father.—

Learning there was like to be Companie at Doctor *Davies'*, I was avised to
put on my brave greene Satin Gown;
and my Husband sayd it became me well,
and that I onlie needed some Primroses
and Cowslips in my Lap, to look like
May;—and somewhat he added about
mine Eyes' "clear shining after Rain,"
which avised me he had perceived I had
beene

beene crying in the Morning, which I had hoped he had not.

Arriving at the Doctor's House, we were shewn into an emptie Chamber ; at least, emptie of Companie, but full of every Thing else ; for there were Books, and Globes, and stringed and wind Instruments, and stuffed Birds and Beasts, and Things I know not soe much as the Names of, besides an Easel with a Painting by Mrs. *Mildred* on it, which she meant to be seene, or she woulde have put it away. Subject, "*Brutus's Judgment :*" which I thought a strange, unfeeling one for a Woman ; and did not wish to be *her* Son. Soone she came in, drest with studdied and puritanicall Plainnesse ; in brown Taffeta, guarded with black Velvet, which became her well enough, but was scarce suited for the Season. She had much to say about limning, in which my Husband could follow her better than I ; and then they went to the Globes, and *Copernicus*, and *Galileo Galilei*, whom she called a Martyr, but I do not. For, is a Martyr

Martyr one who is unwillinglie imprisoned, or who formally recants? even tho' he affecteth afterwards to say 'twas *but* a Form, and cries "*Eppure, si muove?*" The earlier Christians might have sayd 'twas but a Form to burn a Handfull of Incense before *Jove's* Statua; *Pliny* woulde have let them goe.

Afterwards, when the Doctor came in and engaged my Husband in Discourse, Mistress *Mildred* devoted herselfe to me, and askt what Progresse I had made with *Bernardo Tasso*. I tolde her, none at alle, for I was equallie faultie at *Italiques* and *Italian*, and onlie knew his best Work thro' Mr. *Fairfax's* Translation; whereat she fell laughing, and sayd she begged my Forgivenesse, but I was confounding the Father with the Sonne; then laught agayn, but pretended 'twas not at me, but at a Lady I minded her of, who never coulde remember to distinguish betwixt *Lionardo da Vinci* and *Lorenzo dei Medici*. That last Name brought up the Recollection of my Morning's Debate with my Husband, which

which made me feel sad ; and then, Mrs. *Mildred*, seeminge anxious to make me forget her Unmannerliness, commenced, " Can you paint ? "—" Can you sing ? "— " Can you play the Lute ? "—and, at the last, " What *can* you do ? " I mighte have sayd I coulde comb out my Curls smoother than she coulde hers, but did not. Other Guests came in, and talked so much agaynst Prelacy and the Right divine of Kings that I woulde fain we had remained at Astronomie and Poetry. For Supper there was little Meat, and noe strong Drinks, onlie a thinnish foreign Wine, with Cakes, Candies, Sweetmeats, Fruits, and Confections. Such, I suppose, is Town Fashion. At the laste, came Musick ; Mistress *Mildred* sang and played ; then prest me to do the like, but I was soe fearfulle, I coulde not ; so my Husband sayd he woulde play for me, and that woulde be alle one, and soe covered my Bashfullenesse handsomlie.

Onlie this Morning, just before going to his Studdy, he stept back and sayd, " Sweet

"Sweet *Moll*, I know you can both play
"and sing—why will you not practise?"
I replyed, I loved it not much. He rejoyned, "But you know I love it, and is
"not that a Motive?" I sayd, I feared
to let him hear me, I played so ill. He
replyed, "Why, that is the very Reason
"you shoulde seek to play better, and I
"am sure you have Plenty of Time. Per-
"haps, in your whole future Life, you
"will not have such a Season of Leisure
"as you have now,—a golden Opportu-
"nity, which you will surelie seize."—
Then added, "Sir *Thomas More's* Wife
"learnt to play the Lute, solely that she
"mighte please her Husband." I answered, "Nay, what to tell me of Sir
"*Thomas More's* Wife, or of *Hugh Grotius's*
"Wife, when I was the Wife of *John
"Milton?*" He looked at me twice, and
quicklie, too, at this Saying; then laughing, cried, "You cleaving Mischief! I
"hardlie know whether to take that
"Speech amisse or well—however, you
"shall have the Benefit of the Doubt."

          And

And so away laughing ; and I, for very Shame, sat down to the Spinnette for two wearie Hours, till soe tired, I coulde cry ; and when I desisted, coulde hear *Jack* wailing over his Task. 'Tis raining fast, I cannot get out, nor should I dare to go alone, nor where to go to if 'twere fine. I fancy ill Smells from the Churchyard— 'tis long to Dinner-time, with noe Change, noe Exercise ; and oh, I sigh for *Forest Hill*.

—A dull Dinner with Mrs. *Phillips*, whom I like not much. *Christopher Milton* there, who stared hard at me, and put me out of Countenance with his strange Questions. My Husband checked him. He is a Lawyer, and has Wit enoughe.

Mrs. *Phillips* speaking of second Marriages, I unawares hurt her by giving my Voice agaynst them. It seems she is thinking of contracting a second Marriage.

—At Supper, wishing to ingratiate myself with the Boys, talked to them of of Countrie Sports, etc.: to which the youngest listened greedilie: and at length I was advised to ask them woulde they not like to see *Forest Hill?* to which the elder replyed in his most methodicall Manner, "If Mr. *Powell* has a good "Library." For this Piece of Hypocrisie, at which I heartilie laught, he was commended by his Uncle. Hypocrisie it was, for Master *Ned* cryeth over his Taskes pretty nearlie as oft as the youngest.

Friday.

TO rewarde my zealous Practice to-day on the Spinnette, Mr. *Milton* produced a Collection of "*Ayres, and* " *Dialogues, for one, two,* " *and three Voices,*" by his Friend Mr. *Harry Lawes,* which he sayd I shoulde find very pleasant Studdy; and then he told me alle about theire getting up the Masque of *Comus* in *Ludlow* Castle, and how well the Lady's Song was sung by Mr.

F

Mr. *Lawes'* Pupil, the Lady *Alice*, then a sweet, modest Girl, onlie thirteen Yeares of Age,—and he told me of the Singing of a faire *Italian* young Signora, named *Leonora Barroni*, with her Mother and Sister, whome he had hearde at *Rome*, at the Concerts of Cardinal *Barberini;* and how she was "as gentle and modest as "sweet *Moll*," yet not afrayd to open her Mouth, and pronounce everie Syllable distinctlie, and with the proper Emphasis and Passion when she sang. And after this, to my greate Contentment, he tooke me to the *Gray's Inn Walks*, where, the Afternoon being fine, was much Companie.

After Supper, I proposed to the Boys that we shoulde tell Stories; and Mr. *Milton* tolde one charminglie, but then went away to write a *Latin* Letter. Soe *Ned's* Turn came next; and I must, if I can, for very Mirthe's Sake, write it down in his exact Words, they were soe pragmaticall.

"On a Daye, there was a certain Child
"wandered

" wandered forthe, that would play. He
" met a Bee, and sayd, 'Bee, wilt thou
" play with me?' The Bee sayd, 'No,
" I have my Duties to perform, tho' you,
" it woulde seeme, have none. I must
" away to make Honey.' Then the Childe,
" abasht, went to the Ant. He sayd,
" 'Will you play with me, Ant?' The
" Ant replied, 'Nay, I must provide against
" the Winter.' In shorte, he found that
" everie Bird, Beaste, and Insect he ac-
" costed, had a closer Eye to the Purpose
" of their Creation than himselfe. Then
" he sayd, 'I will then back, and con
" my Task.'—*Moral*. The Moral of the
" foregoing Fable, my deare *Aunt*, is this
" —We must love Work better than
Play."

With alle my Interest for Children, how is it possible to take anie Interest in soe formall a little Prigge?

Saturday.

Saturday.

HAVE just done somewhat for Master *Ned* which he coulde not doe for himselfe—*viz.* tenderly bound up his Hand, which he had badly cut. Wiping away some few naturall Tears, he must needs say, " I am quite ashamed, *Aunt*, you shoulde " see me cry ; but the worst of it is, that " alle this Payne has beene for noe good ; " whereas, when my Uncle beateth me " for misconstruing my *Latin*, tho' I cry " at the Time, all the while I know it is " for my Advantage."—If this Boy goes on preaching soe, I shall soon hate him.

—Mr. *Milton* having stepped out before Supper, came back looking soe blythe, that I askt if he had hearde good News. He sayd, yes: that some Friends had long beene persuading him, against his Will, to make publick some of his *Latin* Poems ; and that, having at length consented to theire Wishes, he had beene with *Mosley* the Publisher in *St. Paul's Churchyard*, who

who agreed to print them. I sayd, I was sorrie I shoulde be unable to read them. He sayd he was sorry too; he must trans-

late them for me. I thanked him, but observed that Traductions were never soe good as Originalls. He rejoyned, "Nor
"am

"am I even a good Translater." I askt, "Why not write in your owne Tongue?" He sayd, "*Latin* is understood all over the "Worlde." I sayd, "But there are manie "in your owne Country do not under- "stand it." He was silent soe long upon that, that I supposed he did not mean to answer me; but then cried, "You are "right, sweet *Moll*.—Our best Writers "have written their best Works in *Eng-* "*lish*, and I will hereafter doe the same, "—for I feel that my best Work is still "*to come*. Poetry hath hitherto been with "me rather the Recreation of a Mind "conscious of its Health, than the delibe- "rate Task-work of a Soule that must "hereafter give an Account of its Talents. "Yet my Mind, in the free Circuit of "her Musing, has ranged over a thousand "Themes that lie, like the Marble in the "Quarry, readie for anie Shape that Fancie "and Skill may give. Neither Laziness "nor Caprice makes me difficult in my "Choice; for, the longer I am in select- "ing my Tree, and laying my Axe to the
"Root,

"Root, the sounder it will be and the
"riper for Use. Nor is an Undertaking
"that shall be one of high Duty, to be
"entered upon without Prayer and Dis-
"cipline :— it woulde be Presumption
"indeede, to commence an Enterprise
"which I meant shoulde delighte and
"profit every instructed and elevated
"Mind without so much Paynes-takinge
"as it should cost a poor Mountebank to
"balance a Pole on his Chin."

Sunday Even.

IN the Clouds agayn. At Dinner, to-daye, Mr. *Milton* catechised the Boys on the Morning's Sermon, the Heads of which, though amounting to a Dozen, *Ned* tolde off roundlie. Roguish little *Jack* looked slylie at me, says, "*Aunt* "coulde not tell off the Sermon." "Why "not?" says his Uncle. "Because she "was sleeping," says *Jack*. Provoked with the Child, I turned scarlett, and hastilie

hastilie sayd, "I was not." Nobodie spoke; but I repented the Falsitie the Moment it had escaped me; and there was *Ned*, a folding of his Hands, drawing down his Mouth, and closing his Eyes. . . . My Husband tooke me to taske for it when we were alone, soe tenderlie that I wept.

Monday.

JACK sayd this Morning, "I know Something—I "know *Aunt* keeps a Jour- "nall." "And a good "Thing if you kept one "too, *Jack*," sayd his Uncle, "it would shew you how little "you doe." *Jack* was silenced; but *Ned*, pursing up his Mouth, says, "I can't "think what *Aunt* can have to put in a "Journall—should not you like, *Uncle*, to "see?" "No, *Ned*," says his Uncle, "I "am upon Honour, and your dear Aunt's "Journall is as safe, for me, as the golden "Bracelets that King *Alfred* hung upon "the High-way. I am glad she has such

"a

" a Resource, and, as we know she cannot
" have much News to put in it, we may
" the more safely rely that it is a Treasury
" of sweet, and high, and holy, and profit-
" able Thoughtes."

Oh, how deeplie I blusht at this ill-deserved Prayse! How sorrie I was that I had ever registered aught that he woulde grieve to read! I secretly resolved that this Daye's Journalling should be the last, untill I had attained a better Frame of Mind.

Saturday Even.

HAVE kept Silence, yea, even from good Words, but it has beene a Payn and Griefe unto me. Good Mistress *Catherine Thompson* called on me a few Dayes back, and spoke so wisely and so wholesomelie concerning my Lot, and the Way to make it happy, (she is the first that hath spoken as if 'twere possible it mighte not be soe alreadie,) that I felt for a Season quite heartened; but it has alle faded

faded away. Because the Source of Cheerfulnesse is not *in* me, anie more than in a dull Landskip, which the Sun lighteneth for a while, and when he has set, its Beauty is gone.

Oh me! how merry I was at Home! —The Source of Cheerfulnesse seemed in me *then*, and why is it not *now?* Partly because alle that I was there taught to think right is here thought wrong; because much that I there thought harmlesse is here thought sinfulle; because I cannot get at anie of the Things that employed and interested me *there*, and because the Things within my Reach *here* do not interest me. Then, 'tis no small Thing to be continuallie deemed ignorant and misinformed, and to have one's Errors continuallie covered, however handsomelie, even before Children. To say nothing of the Weight upon the Spiritts at firste, from Change of Ayre, and Diet, and Scene, and Loss of habituall Exercise and Companie and householde Cares. These petty Griefs try me sorelie; and when Cousin *Ralph* came

came in unexpectedlie this Morn, tho' I never much cared for him at Home, yet the Sighte of *Rose's* Brother, fresh from *Sheepscote* and *Oxford* and *Forest Hill*, soe upset me that I sank into Tears. No Wonder that Mr. *Milton*, then coming in, shoulde hastilie enquire if *Ralph* had brought ill Tidings from Home; and, finding alle was well there, shoulde look strangelie. He askt *Ralph*, however, to stay to Dinner; and we had much Talk of Home; but now, I regret having omitted to ask a thousand Questions.

Sunday Even, Aug. 15.

MR. *MILTON* in his Closet and I in my Chamber.— For the first Time he seems this Evening to have founde out how dissimilar are our Minds. Meaning to please him, I sayd, "I kept awake bravelie, to-
" nighte, through that long, long Sermon,
" for your Sake." — " And why not for
" *God's* Sake?" cried he, " why not for
" your

"your owne Sake?—Oh, sweet *Wife*, I
"fear you have yet much to learn of the
"Depth of Happinesse that is comprised
"in the Communion between a forgiven
"Soul and its Creator. It hallows the
"most secular as well as the most spirituall
"Employments; it gives pleasure that has
"no after Bitternesse; it gives Pleasure to
"*God*—and oh! thinke of the Depth of
"Meaning in those Words! think what
"it is for us to be capable of giving *God*
"Pleasure!"

—Much more, in the same Vein! to which I could not, with equal Power, respond; soe, he away to his Studdy, to pray perhaps for my Change of Heart, and I to my Bed.

Aug. 21, *Saturday.*

OH Heaven! can it be possible? am I agayn at *Forest Hill?* How strange, how joyfulle an Event, tho' brought about with Teares! Can it be, that it is onlie a Month since I stoode at this Toilette as

a

a Bride? and lay awake on that Bed, thinking of *London?* How long a Month! and oh! this present one will be alle too short.

It seemeth that *Ralph Hewlett*, shocked at my Teares and the Alteration in my Looks, broughte back a dismall Report of me to deare *Father* and *Mother*, pronouncing me either ill or unhappie. Thereupon, *Richard*, with his usual Impetuositie, prevayled on *Father* to let him and *Ralph* fetch me Home for a While, at leaste till after *Michaelmasse*.

How surprised was I to see *Dick* enter! My Arms were soe fast about his Neck, and my Face prest soe close to his shoulder, that I did not for a While perceive the grave Looke he had put on. At the last, I was avised to ask what broughte him soe unexpectedlie to *London*; and then he hemmed and looked at *Ralph*, and *Ralph* looked at *Dick*, and then *Dick* sayd bluntly, he hoped Mr. *Milton* woulde spare me to go Home till after *Michaelmasse*, and *Father* had sent him on Purpose to say soe.

soe. Mr. *Milton* lookt surprised and hurte, and sayd, how could he be expected to part soe soone with me, a Month's Bride? it must be some other Time: he had intended to take me himselfe to *Forest Hill* the following Spring, but coulde not spare Time now, nor liked me to goe without him, nor thought I should like it myself. But my Eyes said *I shoulde*, and then he gazed earnestlie at me and lookt hurt; and there was a dead Silence. Then *Dick*, hesitating a little, sayd he was sorrie to tell us my *Father* was ill; on which I clasped my Hands and beganne to weepe; and Mr. *Milton*, changing Countenance, askt sundrie Questions, which *Dick* answered well enough; and then said he woulde not be soe cruel as to keepe me from a Father I soe dearlie loved, if he were sick, though he liked not my travelling in such unsettled Times with so young a Convoy. *Ralph* sayd they had brought *Diggory* with them, who was olde and steddy enough, and had ridden my *Mother's* Mare for my Use; and *Dick* was for our getting

getting forward a Stage on our Journey the same Evening, but Mr. *Milton* insisted on our abiding till the following Morn, and woulde not be overruled. And gave me leave to stay a Month, and gave me Money, and many kind Words, which I coulde mark little, being soe overtaken with Concern about dear *Father*, whose Illness I feared to be worse than *Dick* sayd, seeing he seemed soe close and dealt in dark Speeches and Parables. After Dinner, they went forth, they sayd, to look after the Horses, but I think to see *London*, and returned not till Supper.

We got them Beds in a House hard by, and started at earlie Dawn.

Mr. *Milton* kissed me most tenderlie agayn and agayn at parting, as though he feared to lose me; but it had seemed to me soe hard to brook the Delay of even a few Hours when *Father*, in his Sicknesse, was wanting me, that I took leave of my Husband with less Affection than I mighte have shewn, and onlie began to find my Spiritts lighten when we were fairly quit
of

of *London* with its vile Sewers and Drains, and to breathe the sweete, pure Morning Ayre, as we rode swiftlie along. *Dick* called *London* a vile Place, and spake to *Ralph* concerning what they had seene of it overnighte, whence it appeared to me, that he had beene pleasure-seeking more than, in *Father's* state, he ought to have beene. But *Dick* was always a reckless Lad;—and oh, what Joy, on reaching this deare Place, to find *Father* had onlie beene suffering under one of his usual Stomach Attacks, which have no Danger in them, and which *Dick* had exaggerated, fearing Mr. *Milton* woulde not otherwise part with me;—I was a little shocked, and coulde not help scolding him, though I was the gainer; but he boldlie defended what he called his "Stratagem of War," saying it was quite allowable in dealing with a *Puritan*.

As for *Robin*, he was wild with Joy when I arrived; and hath never ceased to hang about me. The other Children are riotous in their Mirth. Little *Joscelyn* hath

hath returned from his Foster-mother's Farm, and is noe longer a puny Child—'tis thought he will thrive. I have him constantly in my Arms or riding on my Shoulder; and with Delight have revisited alle my olde Haunts, patted *Clover*, &c. Deare *Mother* is most kind. The Maids as oft call me Mrs. *Molly* as Mrs. *Milton*, and then smile, and beg Pardon. *Rose* and *Agnew* have been here, and have made me promise to visit *Sheepscote* before I return to *London*. The whole House seems full of Glee.

Monday.

IT seemes quite strange to heare *Dick* and *Harry* singing loyal Songs and drinking the *King's* Health after soe recentlie hearing his M. soe continuallie spoken agaynst. Also, to see a Lad of *Robin's* Age, coming in and out at his Will, doing aniething or nothing; instead of being ever at his Taskes, and looking at at Meal-times as if he were repeating them to himselfe. I know which I like best.

A most kind Letter from Mr. *Milton*, hoping *Father* is better, and praying for News of him. How can I write to him without betraying *Dick?* *Robin* and I rode, this Morning, to *Sheepscote*. Thoughte Mr. *Agnew* received me with unwonted Gravitie. He tolde me he had received a Letter from my Husband, praying news of my Father, seeing I had sent him none, and that he had writ to him that *Father* was quite well, never had been better. Then he sayd to me he feared Mr. *Milton* was labouring under some false Impression. I tolde him trulie, that *Dick*, to get me Home, had exaggerated a trifling Illness of *Father's*, but that I was guiltlesse of it. He sayd *Dick* was inexcusable, and that noe good End coulde justifie a Man of Honour in overcharging the Truth; and that, since I was innocent, I shoulde write to my Husband to clear myself. I said briefly, I woulde; and I mean to do soe, onlie

onlie not to-daye. Oh, sweet countrie Life! I was made for you and none other. This riding and walking at one's owne free Will, in the fresh pure Ayre, coming in to earlie, heartie, wholesome Meals, seasoned with harmlesse Jests, — seeing fresh Faces everie Daye come to the House, knowing everie Face one meets out of Doores, — supping in the Garden, and remaining in the Ayre long after the Moon has risen, talking, laughing, or perhaps dancing,—if this be not Joyfulnesse, what is?

For certain, I woulde that Mr. *Milton* were here; but he woulde call our Sports mistimed, and throw a Damp upon our Mirth by not joining in it. Soe I will enjoy my Holiday while it lasts, for it may be long ere I get another—especiallie if his and *Father's* opinions get wider asunder, as I think they are doing alreadie. My promised Spring Holiday may come to nothing.

Monday.

Monday.

MY Husband hath writ to me strangelie, chiding me most unkindlie for what was noe Fault of mine, to wit, *Dick's* Falsitie; and wondering I can derive anie Pleasure from a Holiday so obtayned, which he will not curtayl, but will on noe Pretence extend. Nay! but methinks Mr. *Milton* presumeth somewhat too much on his marital Authoritie, writing in this Strayn. I am no mere Child neither, nor a runaway Wife, nor in such bad Companie, in mine own Father's House, where he firste saw me; and, was it anie Fault of mine, indeed, that *Father* was not ill? or can I wish he had beene? No, truly!

This Letter hath sorelie vexed me. Dear *Father*, seeing me soe dulle, askt me if I had had bad News. I sayd I had, for that Mr. *Milton* wanted me back at the Month's End. He sayd, lightlie, Oh, that

that must not be, I must at all Events stay over his Birthdaye, he could not spare me sooner; he woulde settle all that. Let it be soe then—I am content enoughe.

To change the Current of my Thoughts, he hath renewed the Scheme for our Visit to Lady *Falkland*, which, Weather permitting, is to take Place to-morrow. 'Tis long since I have seene her, soe I am willing to goe; but she is dearer to *Rose* than to me, though I respect her much.

Wednesday.

THE whole of Yesterday occupyde with our Visitt. I love Lady *Falkland* well, yet her religious Mellanchollie and Presages of Evil have left a Weight upon my Spiritts. To-daye, we have a Family Dinner. The *Agnews* come not, but the *Merediths* doe, we shall have more Mirthe if less Wit. My Time now draweth

draweth soe short, I must crowd into it alle the Pleasure I can; and in this, everie one conspires to help me, saying, "Poor *Moll* must soon return to *London*." Never was Creature soe petted or spoylt. How was it there was none of this before I married, when they might have me alwaies? ah, therein lies the Secret. Now, we have mutuallie tasted our Losse.

Ralph Hewlett, going agayn to Town, was avised to ask whether I had anie Commission wherewith to charge him. I bade him tell Mr. *Milton* that since we should meet soe soone, I need not write, but would keep alle my News for our Fire-side. *Robin* added, " Say, we cannot " spare her yet," and *Father* echoed the same.

But I begin to feel now, that I must not prolong my Stay. At the leaste, not beyond *Father's* Birthday. My Month is hasting to a Close.

Sept.

Sept. 21.

BATTLE at *Newbury*—Lord *Falkland* slayn. Oh, fatal Loss! *Father* and *Mother* going off to my Lady: but I think she will not see them. Aunt and Uncle *Hewlett*, who brought the News, can talk of nothing else.

Sept. 22.

ALLE Sadnesse and Consternation. I am wearie of bad News, public and private, and feel less and less Love for the Puritans, yet am forced to seem more loyal than I really am, soe high runs party Feeling just now at Home.

My Month has passed!

Sept. 28.

MOST displeased Letter from my Husband, minding me that my Leave of Absence hath expired, and that he likes not the Messages he received through *Ralph*, nor the unreasonable and hurtfulle Pastimes which he finds have beene making my quiet Home distastefulle. Asking, are they suitable, under Circumstances of nationall Consternation to *my owne* Party, or seemlie in soe young a Wife, apart from her Husband? To conclude, insisting, with more Authoritie than Kindnesse, on my immediate Return.

With Tears in my Eyes, I have beene to my Father. I have tolde him I must goe. He sayeth, Oh no, not yet. I persisted, I must, my Husband was soe very angry. He rejoined, What, angry with my sweet *Moll*? and for spending a few Days with her old Father? Can it be? hath it come to this alreadie?
I

I sayd, my Month had expired. He sayd, Nonsense, he had always askt me to stay over *Michaelmasse*, till his Birthday; he knew *Dick* had named it to Mr. *Milton*. I sayd, Mr. *Milton* had taken no Notice thereof, but had onlie granted me a Month. He grew peevish, and said "Pooh, pooh!" Thereat, after a Silence of a Minute or two, I sayd yet agayn, I must goe. He took me by the two Wrists and sayd, Doe you wish to go? I burst into Teares, but made noe Answer. He sayd, That is Answer enough, —how doth this Puritan carry it with you, my Child? and snatched his Letter. I sayd, Oh, don't read that, and would have drawn it back; but *Father*, when heated, is impossible to controwl; therefore, quite deaf to Entreaty, he would read the Letter, which was unfit for him in his chafed Mood; then, holding it at Arm's Length, and smiting it with his Fist,—Ha! and is it thus he dares address a Daughter of mine? (with Words added, I dare not write)—but be quiet, *Moll*, be

at

at Peace, my Child, for he shall not have you back for awhile, even though he come to fetch you himself. The maddest Thing I ever did was to give you to this Roundhead. He and *Roger Agnew* talked me over in soe many fine Words.—What possessed me, I know not. Your Mother always said evil woulde come of it. But as long as thy Father has a Roof over his Head, Child, thou hast a Home.

As soone as he woulde hear me, I begged him not to take on soe, for that I was not an unhappy Wife; but my Tears, he sayd, belied me; and indeed, with Fear and Agitation, they flowed fast enough. But I sayd, I *must* goe home, and wished I had gone sooner, and woulde he let *Diggory* take me! No, he sayd, not a Man Jack on his Land shoulde saddle a Horse for me, nor would he lend me one, to carry me back to Mr. *Milton;* at the leaste not for a While, till he had come to Reason, and protested he was sorry for having writ to me soe harshly.

" Soe be content, *Moll*, and make
" not

"At Squire Foxes's Grand Dinner"

"not two Enemies instead of one. Goe,
"help thy Mother with her clear-starch-
"ing. Be happy whilst thou art here."

But ah! more easily said than done.
"Alle Joy is darkened; the Mirthe of
"the Land is gone!"

Michaelmasse Day.

AT Squire *Paice's* grand Dinner we have been counting on soe many Days; but it gave me not the Pleasure expected.

Oct. 13.

THE Weather is soe foul that I am sure Mr. *Milton* woulde not like me to be on the Road, even would my Father let me goe.

—While writing the above, heard very angrie Voices in the Court-yard, my Father's especiallie, louder than common; and distinguished the

the words "Knave," and "Varlet," and "begone." Lookt from my Window and beheld a Man, booted and cloaked, with two Horses, at the Gate, parleying with my Father, who stood in an offensive Attitude, and woulde not let him in. I could catch such Fragments as, "But, "Sir!" "What! in such Weather as "this?" "Nay, it had not overcast "when I started." "'Tis foul enough "now, then." "Let me but have speech "of my Mistress." "You crosse not my "Threshold." "Nay, Sir, if but to give "her this Letter:"—and turning his Head, I was avised of its being *Hubert*, old Mr. *Milton's* Man; doubtless sent by my Husband to fetch me. Seeing my Father raise his Hand in angrie Action (his Riding-whip being in it), I hasted down as fast as I coulde, to prevent Mischiefe, as well as to get my Letter; but, unhappilie, not soe fleetlie as to see more than *Hubert's* flying Skirts as he gallopped from the Gate, with the led Horse by the Bridle; while my Father flinging

flinging downe the torne Letter, walked passionatelie away. I clasped my Hands, and stood mazed for a while,—was then avised to piece the Letter, but could not; onlie making out such Words as "Sweet *Moll*," in my Husband's Writing.

Oct. 14.

ROSE came this Morning, through Rain and Mire, at some Risk as well as much Inconvenience, to intreat of me, even with Teares, not to vex Mr. *Milton* by anie further Delays, but to return to him as soon as possible. Kind Soule, her Affection toucht me, and I assured her the more readilie I intended to return Home as soone as I coulde, which was not yet, my Father having taken the Matter into his own Hands, and permitting me noe Escort; but that I questioned not, Mr. *Milton* was onlie awaiting the Weather to settle, to fetch me himself. That he he will doe so, is my firm Persuasion. Meanwhile, I make it my Duty to joyn with some Attempt at Cheerfulnesse in the Amusements of others, to make my Father's Confinement to the House less irksome; and have in some Measure succeeded.

Oct. 23.

NOE Sighte nor Tidings of Mr. *Milton.* — I am uneasie, frighted at myself, and wish I had never left him, yet hurte at the Neglect. *Hubert,* being a crabbed Temper, made Mischief on his Return, I fancy. *Father* is vexed, methinks, at his owne Passion, and hath never, directlie, spoken, in my Hearinge, of what passed; but rayleth continuallie agaynst Rebels and Roundheads. As to *Mother,*—ah me.

Oct.

Oct. 24.

HRO' dank and miry Lanes and Bye-roads with *Robin*, to *Sheepscote*.

Waiting for *Rose* in Mr. *Agnew's* small Studdy, where she mostlie sitteth with him, oft acting as his Amanuensis, was avised to take up a printed Sheet of Paper that lay on the Table; but finding it to be of *Latin* Versing, was about to laye it downe agayn, when *Rose* came in. She changed Colour, and in a faltering Voice sayd, "Ah, *Cousin*, do you know "what that is? One of your Husband's "Proofe Sheets. I woulde that it coulde "interest you in like manner as it hath "me." Made her noe Answer, laying it aside unconcernedlie, but secretlie felt, as I have oft done before, how stupid it is not to know *Latin*, and resolved to get *Robin* to teach me. He is noe greate Scholar himselfe, soe will not shame me. —I am wearie of hearing of War and Politicks;

Politicks; soe will try Studdy for a while, and see if 'twill cure this dull Payn at my Heart.

Oct. 28.

ROBIN and I have shut ourselves up for three Hours dailie, in the small Bookroom, and have made fayre Progresse. He liketh his Office of Tutor mightilie.

Oct. 31.

MY Lessons are more crabbed, or I am more dull and inattentive, for I cannot fix my Minde on my Book, and am secretlie wearie. *Robin* wearies too. But I will not give up as yet; the more soe as in this quiete Studdy I am out of Sighte and Hearinge of sundrie young Officers *Dick* is continuallie bringing over from *Oxford*, who spend manie Hours with him in Countrie Sports, and then come into

into the House, hungry, thirstie, noisie, and idle. I know Mr. *Milton* woulde not like them.

—Surelie he will come soone?—I sayd to *Father* last Night, I wanted to hear from Home. He sayd, "Home! Dost call "yon Taylor's Shop your Home?" soe ironicalle that I was shamed to say more.

Woulde that I had never married!— then coulde I enjoy my Childhoode's Home. Yet I knew not its Value before I quitted it, and had even a stupid Pleasure in anticipating another. Ah me! had I loved Mr. *Milton* more, perhaps I might better have endured the Taylor's Shop.

Sheepscote, Nov. 20.

ANNOYED by *Dick's* companions, I prayed *Father* to let me stay awhile with *Rose*; and gaining his Consent, came over here Yester-morn, without thinking it needfulle to send Notice, which was perhaps

perhaps inconsiderate. But she received me with Kisses and Words of Tendernesse, though less Smiling than usualle, and eagerlie accepted mine offered Visitt. Then she ran off to find *Roger*, and I heard them talking earnestlie in a low Voice before they came in. His Face was grave, even stern, when he entred, but he held out his Hand, and sayd, " Mistress *Milton*, you are welcome! how " is it with you? and how was Mr. " *Milton* when he wrote to you last?" I answered brieflie, he was well: then came a Silence, and then *Rose* took me to my Chamber, which was sweet with Lavender, and its hangings of the whitest. It reminded me too much of my first Week of Marriage, soe I resolved to think not at all lest I shoulde be bad Companie, but cheer up and be gay. Soe I askt *Rose* a thousand Questions about her Dairie and Bees, laught much at Dinner, and told Mr. *Agnew* sundrie of the merrie Sayings of *Dick* and his *Oxford* Friends. And, for my Reward, when

when we were afterwards apart, I heard him tell *Rose* (by Reason of the Walls being thin) that however she might regard me for old Affection's sake, he thought he had never knowne soe unpromising a Character. This made me dulle enoughe all the rest of the Evening, and repent having come to *Sheepscote:* however, he liked me the better for being quiete: and *Rose*, being equallie chekt, we sewed in Silence while he read to us the first Division of *Spencer's Legend of Holinesse*, about *Una* and the Knight, and how they got sundered. This led to much serious, yet not unpleasing, Discourse, which lasted till Supper. For the first Time at *Sheepscote*, I coulde not eat, which Mr. *Agnew* observing, prest me to take Wine, and *Rose* woulde start up to fetch some of her Preserves; but I chekt her with a Motion, not being quite able to speak; for their being soe kind made the Teares ready to starte, I knew not why.

Family Prayers, after Supper, rather too long; yet though I coulde not keep up up my Attention, they seemed to spread a Calm and a Peace alle about, that extended even to me; and though, after I had undressed, I sat a long while in a Maze, and bethought me how piteous a Creature I was, yet, once layed down, I never sank into deeper, more composing Sleep.

Nov. 21.

THIS Morning, *Rose* exclaimed, " Dear *Roger!* " onlie think! *Moll* has " begun to learn *Latin* " since she returned to " *Forest Hill*, thinking to " surprise Mr. *Milton* when they meet." " She will not onlie surprise but *please* " him," returned dear *Roger*, taking my Hand very kindlie; " I can onlie say, I " hope they will meet long before she " can read his *Poemata*, unless she learnes " much faster than most People." I replyed, I learned very slowly, and wearied *Robin's* Patience; on which *Rose*, kissing me, me, cried, " You will never wearie mine; "soe, if you please, deare *Moll,* we will "goe to our Lessons here everie Morn-"ing; and it may be that I shall get you "through the Grammar faster than *Robin* "can. If we come to anie Difficultie we "shall refer it to *Roger.*"

Now, Mr. *Agnew's* Looks exprest such Pleasure with both, that it were difficult to tell which felt the most elated; soe calling me deare *Moll* (he hath hitherto Mistress *Miltoned* me ever since I sett Foot in his House), he sayd he would not interrupt our Studdies, though he should be within Call, and soe left us. I had not felt soe happy since *Father's* Birthday; and, though *Rose* kept me close to my Book for two Hours, I found her a far less irksome Tutor than deare *Robin.* Then she went away, singing, to make *Roger's* favourite Dish, and afterwards we took a brisk Walke, and came Home hungrie enoughe to Dinner.

There is a daily Beauty in *Rose's* Life, that I not onlie admire, but am readie to envy.

envy. Oh! if *Milton* lived but in the poorest House in the Countrie, methinks I coulde be very happy with him.

Bedtime.

CHANCING to make the above Remark to *Rose*, she cried, "And why not be "happy with him in *Al-* "*dersgate Street?*" I briefly replied that he must get the House first, before it were possible to tell whether I coulde be happy there or not. *Rose* stared, and exclaimed, "Why, where do you suppose him to be "now?" "Where but at the Taylor's "in *St. Bride's Churchyard?*" I replied. She claspt her Hands with a Look I shall never forget, and exclaimed in a sort of vehement Passion, "Oh, *Cousin, Cousin,* "how you throw your own Happinesse "away! How awfulle a Pause must "have taken place in your Intercourse "with the Man whom you promised to "abide by till Death, since you know "not

" not that he has long since taken posses-
" sion of his new Home; that he strove
" to have it ready for you at *Michael-*
" *masse!* "

Doubtlesse I lookt noe less surprised
than I felt;—a suddain Prick at the
Heart prevented Speech; but it shot
acrosse my Heart that I had made out the
Words " Aldersgate " and " new Home,"
in the Fragments of the Letter my Father
had torn. *Rose*, misjudging my Silence,
burst forth anew with, " Oh, *Cousin!*
" *Cousin!* coulde anie Home, however
" dull and noisesome, drive me from
" *Roger Agnew?* Onlie think of what
" you are doing,—of what you are leav-
" ing undone!—of what you are pre-
" paring against yourself! To put the
" Wickednesse of a selfish Course out of
" the Account, onlie think of its Mellan-
" cholie, its Miserie,—destitute of alle
" the sweet, bright, fresh Wellsprings of
" Happinesse;—unblest by *God!* "

Here *Rose* wept passionatelie, and claspt
her Arms about me; but, when I began
to

to speak, and to tell her of much that had made me miserable, she hearkened in motionlesse Silence, till I told her that *Father* had torn the Letter and beaten the Messenger. Then she cried, "Oh, I "see now what may and shall be done! "*Roger* shall be Peacemaker," and ran off with Joyfulnesse; I not withholding her. But I can never be joyfulle more— he cannot be Day's-man betwixt us now —'tis alle too late!

Nov. 28.

NOW that I am at *Forest Hill* agayn, I will essay to continue my Journalling.—

Mr. *Agnew* was out; and though a keene wintry Wind was blowing, and *Rose* was suffering from Colde, yet she went out to listen for his Horse's Feet at the Gate, with onlie her Apron cast over her Head. Shortlie, he returned; and I heard him say in a troubled Voice, "Alle "are in Arms at *Forest Hill*." I felt soe greatlie

greatlie shocked as to neede to sit downe instead of running forthe to learn the News. I supposed the parliamentarian Soldiers had advanced, unexpectedlie, upon *Oxford.* His next Words were, " *Dick* is coming for her at Noone—poor " Soul, I know not what she will doe— " her Father will trust her noe longer " with you and me." Then I saw them both passe the Window, slowlie pacing together, and hastened forth to joyn them; but they had turned into the pleached Alley, their Backs towards me; and both in such earnest and apparentlie private Communication, that I dared not interrupt them till they turned aboute, which was not for some While; for they stood for some Time at the Head of the Alley, still with theire Backs to me, *Rose's* Hair blowing in the cold Wind; and once or twice she seemed to put her Kerchief to her Eyes.

Now, while I stood mazed and uncertain, I hearde a distant Clatter of Horse's Feet, on the hard Road a good way off, and

and could descrie *Dick* coming towards *Sheepscote*. *Rose* saw him too, and commenced running towards me; Mr. *Agnew* following with long Strides. *Rose* drew me back into the House, and sayd, kissing me, " Dearest *Moll*, I am soe sorry;
" *Roger* hath seen your Father this Morn,
" and he will on no Account spare you
" to us anie longer; and *Dick* is coming
" to fetch you even now." I sayd, " Is
" *Father* ill?" "Oh no," replied Mr. *Agnew*; then coming up, "He is not ill,
" but he is perturbed at something which
" has occurred; and, in Truth, soe am I.
" —But remember, Mistress *Milton*, re-
" member, dear *Cousin*, that when you
" married, your *Father's* Guardianship of
" you passed into the Hands of your
" Husband—your Husband's House was
" thenceforthe your Home; and in quit-
" ting it you committed a Fault you may
" yet repaire, though this offensive Act
" has made the Difficultie much greater."
—" Oh, what has happened?" I impatientlie cried. Just then, *Dick* comes in
with

with his usual blunt Salutations, and then cries, "Well, *Moll*, are you ready to goe "back?" "Why should I be?" I sayd, "when I am soe happy here? unless "*Father* is ill, or Mr. *Agnew* and *Rose* "are tired of me." They both interrupted, there was nothing they soe much desired, at this present, as that I shoulde prolong my Stay. And you know, *Dick*, I added, that *Forest Hill* is not soe pleasant to me just now as it hath commonlie beene, by Reason of your *Oxford* Companions. He brieflie sayd, I neede not mind that, they were coming no more to the House, *Father* had decreed it. And you know well enough, *Moll*, that what *Father* decrees, must be, and he hath decreed that you must come Home now; soe no more Ado, I pray you, but fetch your Cloak and Hood, and the Horses shall come round, for 'twill be late ere we reach Home. "Nay, you must dine "here at all Events," sayd *Rose;* "I know, "*Dick*, you love roast Pork." Soe *Dick* relented. Soe *Rose*, turning to me, prayed me me to bid *Cicely* hasten Dinner; the which I did, tho' thinking it strange *Rose* should not goe herself. But, as I returned, I hearde her say, Not a Word of it, dear *Dick*, at the least, till after Dinner, lest you spoil her Appetite. Soe *Dick* sayd he shoulde goe and look after the Horses. I sayd then, brisklie, I see somewhat is the Matter—pray tell me what it is. But *Rose* looked quite dull, and walked to the Window. Then, Mr. *Agnew* sayd, " You seem as dissatisfied to " leave us, *Cousin*, as we are to lose you; " and yet you are going back to *Forest* " *Hill*—to that Home in which you will " doubtlesse be happy to live all your " Dayes."—" At *Forest Hill?* " I sayd, " oh no! I hope not." "And why?" sayd he quicklie. I hung my Head, and muttered, " I hope, some Daye, to goe " back to Mr. *Milton*." " And why not " at once?" sayd he. I sayd, " *Father* " would not let me." " Nay, that is " childish," he answered, " your Father " could not hinder you if you wanted not " the

"the Mind to goe—it was your first
"seeming soe loth to return, that made
"him think you unhappie and refuse to
"part with you." I sayd, "And what if
"I were unhappie?" He paused; and
knew not at the Moment what Answer
to make, but shortlie replyed by another
Question, "What Cause had you to be
"soe?" I sayd, "That was more easily
"askt than answered, even if there were
"anie Neede I shoulde answer it, or he
"had anie Right to ask it." He cried
in an Accent of Tendernesse that still
wrings my Heart to remember, "Oh,
"question not the Right! I only wish
"to make you happy. Were you not
"happy with Mr. *Milton* during the
"Week you spent together here at *Sheeps-*
"*cote?*" Thereat I coulde not refrayn
from bursting into Tears. *Rose* now
sprang forward; but Mr. *Agnew* sayd,
"Let her weep, let her weep, it will do
"her good." Then, alle at once it occurred to me that my Husband was awaiting me at Home, and I cried, "Oh, is
"Mr.

"Mr. *Milton* at *Forest Hill?*" and felt my Heart full of Gladness. Mr. *Agnew* answered, "Not soe, not soe, poor *Moll:*" and, looking up at him, I saw him wiping his Brow, though the Daye was soe chill. "As well tell her now," sayd he to *Rose;* and then taking my Hand, "Oh, "Mrs. *Milton*, can you wonder that your "Husband should be angry? How can "you wonder at anie Evil that may result "from the Provocation you have given "him? What Marvell, that since you "cast him off, all the sweet Fountains of "his Affections would be embittered, and "that he should retaliate by seeking a "Separation, and even a Divorce?"— There I stopt him with an outcry of "Divorce?" "Even soe," he most mournfully replyed, "and I seeke not to "excuse him, since two Wrongs make "not a Right." "But," I cried, passionately weeping, "I have given him noe "Cause; my Heart has never for a Mo-"ment strayed to another, nor does he, I "am sure, expect it." "Ne'erthelesse," enjoyned

enjoyned Mr. *Agnew*, "He is soe aggrieved "and chafed, that he has followed up "what he considers your Breach of the "Marriage Contract by writing and pub- "lishing a Book on Divorce; the Tenor "of which coming to your Father's Ears, "has violently incensed him. And now, "dear *Cousin*, having, by your Wayward- "ness, kindled this Flame, what remains "for you but to—nay, hear me, hear me, "*Moll*, for *Dick* is coming in, and I may "not let him hear me urge you to the "onlie Course that can regayn your Peace "—Mr. *Milton* is still your Husband; "eache of you have now Something to "forgive; do you be the firste; nay, "seeke *his* Forgivenesse, and you shall "be happier than you have been yet."

—But I was weeping without controule; and *Dick* coming in, and with *Dick* the Dinner, I askt to be excused, and soe soughte my Chamber, to weep there without Restraynt or Witnesse. Poor *Rose* came up, as soone as she coulde leave the Table, and told me she had
eaten

eaten as little as I, and woulde not even presse me to eat. But she carest me and comforted me, and urged in her owne tender Way alle that had beene sayd by Mr. *Agnew;* even protesting that if she were in my Place, she woulde not goe back to *Forest Hill,* but straight to *London,* to entreat with Mr. *Milton* for his Mercy. But I told her I could not do that, even had I the means for the Journey; for that my Heart was turned against the Man who coulde, for the venial Offence of a young Wife, in abiding too long with her old Father, not onlie cast her off from his Love, but hold her up to the World's Blame and Scorn, by making their domestic Quarrel the Matter for a printed Attack. *Rose* sayd, "I admit he is "wrong, but indeed, indeed, *Moll,* you "are wrong too, and you were wrong "*first:*" and she sayd this soe often, that at length we came to crosser Words; when *Dick,* calling to me from below, would have me make haste, which I was glad to doe, and left *Sheepscote* less regrettfullie

fullie than I had expected. *Rose* kist me with her gravest Face. Mr. *Agnew* put me on my Horse, and sayd, as he gave me the Rein, " Now think ! now think ! " even yet ! " and then, as I silently rode off, " *God* bless you."

I held down my Head ; but, at the Turn of the Road, lookt back, and saw him and *Rose* watching us from the Porch. *Dick* cried, " I am righte glad " we are off at last, for *Father* is down- " right crazie aboute this Businesse, and " mistrustfulle of *Agnew's* influence over " you,"—and would have gone on railing, but I bade him for Pitie's Sake be quiete.

The Effects of my owne Follie, the Losse of Home, Husband, Name, the Opinion of the *Agnews*, the Opinion of the Worlde, rose up agaynst me and almost drove me mad. And, just as I was thinking I had better lived out my Dayes and dyed earlie in *St. Bride's Churchyarde* than that alle this should have come about, the sudden Recollection of what
Rose

Rose had that Morning tolde me, which soe manie other Thoughts had driven out of my Head, viz. that Mr. *Milton* had, in his Desire to please me, while I was onlie bent on pleasing myself, been secretly striving to make readie the *Aldersgate Street* House agaynst my Return,—soe overcame me, that I wept as I rode along. Nay, at the Corner of a branch Road, had a Mind to beg *Dick* to let me goe to *London;* but a glance at his dogged Countenance sufficed to foreshow my Answer.

Half dead with Fatigue and Griefe when I reached Home, the tender Embraces of my Father and Mother completed the Overthrowe of my Spiritts. I tooke to my Bed; and this is the first Daye I have left it; nor will they let me send for *Rose*, nor even tell her I am ill.

Jan. 1, 1644.

THE new Year opens drearilie, on Affairs both publick and private. The Loaf parted at Breakfast this Morning, which, as the Saying goes, is a Sign of Separation; but *Mother* onlie sayd 'twas because it was badly kneaded, and chid *Margery*. She hath beene telling me, but now, how I mighte have 'scaped all my Troubles, and seene as much as I woulde of her and *Father*, and yet have contented Mr. *Milton* and beene counted a good Wife. Noe Advice soe ill to bear as that which comes too late.

Jan. 7.

I AM sick of this journalling, soe shall onlie put downe the Date of *Robin's* leaving Home. *Lord* have Mercy on him, and keepe him in Safetie. This is a shorte Prayer; therefore, easier to be often

often repeated. When he kissed me, he whispered, "*Moll*, pray for me."

Jan. 27.

FATHER does not seeme to miss *Robin* much, tho' he dailie drinks his Health after that of the King. Perhaps he did not miss me anie more when I was in *London*, though it was true and naturall enough he should like to see me agayn. We should have beene used to our Separation by this Time; there would have beene nothing corroding in it. . . .

I pray for *Robin* everie Night. Since he went, the House has lost its Sunshine. When I was soe anxious to return to *Forest Hill*, I never counted on his leaving it.

Feb.

Feb. 1.

OH Heaven, what would I give to see the Skirts of Mr. *Milton's* Garments agayn! My Heart is sick unto Death. I have been reading some of my *Journall*, and tearing out much childish Nonsense at the Beginning; but coulde not destroy the painfulle Records of the last Year. How unhappy a Creature am I! —wearie, wearie of my Life, yet no Ways inclined for Death. *Lord*, have Mercy upon me.

March 27.

I SPEND much of my Time, now, in the Book-room, and though I essay not to pursue the *Latin*, I read much *English*, at the least, more than ever I did in my Life before; but often I fancy I am reading when I am onlie dreaming. *Oxford* is far too gay a Place for me now ever

ever to goe neare it, but my Brothers are much there, and *Father* in his Farm, and *Mother* in her Kitchen ; and the Neighbours, when they call, look on me strangelie, so that I have noe Love for them. How different is *Rose's* holy, secluded, yet cheerfulle Life at *Sheepscote !* She hath a Nurserie now, soe cannot come to me, and *Father* likes not I should goe to her.

April 5.

THEY say their Majestyes' Parting at *Abingdon* was very sorrowfulle and tender. The *Lord* send them better Times! The Queen is to my Mind a most charming Lady, and well worthy of his Majesty's Affection ; yet it seems to me amisse, that thro' her Influence, last Summer, the Opportunitie of Pacification was lost. But she was elated, and naturallie enoughe, at her personall Successes from the Time of her landing. To me, there

seems

seems nothing soe good as Peace. I know, indeede, Mr. *Milton* holds that there may be such Things as a holy War and a cursed Peace.

April 10.

FATHER, having a Hoarseness, hath deputed me, of late, to read the Morning and Evening Prayers. How beautifulle is our Liturgie! I grudge at the Puritans for having abolished it; and though I felt not its comprehensive Fullnesse before I married, nor indeed till now, yet I wearied to Death in *London* at the puritanicall Ordinances and Conscience-meetings and extempore Prayers, wherein it was soe oft the Speaker's Care to show Men how godly he was. Nay, I think Mr. *Milton* altogether wrong in the View he takes of praying to *God* in other Men's Words; for doth he not doe soe, everie Time he followeth the Sense of another Man's extempore Prayer, wherein he he is more at his Mercy and Caprice than when he hath a printed Form set down, wherein he sees what is coming?

June 8.

WALKING in the Home-close this Morning, it occurred to me that Mr. *Milton* intended bringing me to *Forest Hill* about this Time; and that if I had abided patientlie with him through the Winter, we might now have beene both here happily together; untroubled by that Sting which now poisons everie Enjoyment of mine, and perhaps of his. *Lord*, be merciful to *me a Sinner*.

June 23.

JUST after writing the above, I was in the Garden, gathering a few Coronation Flowers and Sops-in-Wine, and thinking they were of deeper Crimson at *Sheepscote*, and wondering what *Rose* was just then

then about, and whether, had I beene born in her Place, I shoulde have beene as goode and happy as she,—when *Harry* came up, looking somewhat grave. I sayd, " What is the Matter ? " He gave Answer, "*Rose* hath lost her Child." Oh ! ——that we should live but a two Hours' Journey apart, and that she coulde lose a Child three Months olde *whom I had never seene !*

I ran to *Father*, and never left off praying him to let me goe to her till he consented.

—What, and if I had begged as hard, at the firste, to goe back to Mr. *Milton ?* might he not have consented *then ?*

. . . Soe *Harry* took me ; and as we drew neare *Sheepscote*, I was avised to think how grave, how barely friendly had beene our last Parting ; and to ponder, would *Rose* make me welcome now ? The Infant, *Harry* tolde me, had beene dead some Dayes ; and, as we came in Sight of the little grey old Church, we saw a Knot of People coming out of the Church-yard,

yard, and guessed the Baby had just beene buried. Soe it proved—Mr. *Agnew's* House-door stood ajar; and when we tapped softlie and *Cicely* admitted us, we could see him standing by *Rose*, who was sitting on the Ground and crying as if she would not be comforted. When she hearde my Voice, she started up, flung her Arms about me, crying more bitterlie than before, and I cried too; and Mr. *Agnew* went away with *Harry*. Then *Rose* sayd to me, "You must not leave "me agayn." . . .

. . . In the Cool of the Evening, when *Harry* had left us, she took me into the Churchyarde, and scattered the little Grave with Flowers; and then continued sitting beside it on the Grasse, quiete, but not comfortlesse. I am avised to think she prayed. Then Mr. *Agnew* came forthe and sate on a flat Tombstone hard by; and without one Word of Introduction took out his *Psalter*, and commenced reading the Psalms for that Evening's Service; to wit, the 41st, the 42d, the 43de;

"Then Mr Agnew came and sot on a flat Tomb stone"

43de; in a low solemne Voice; and methoughte I never in my Life hearde aniething to equall it in the Way of Consolation. *Rose's* heavie Eyes graduallie lookt up from the Ground into her Husband's Face, and thence up to Heaven. After this, he read, or rather repeated, the Collect at the end of the Buriall Service, putting this Expression,—" As our " Hope is, this our deare Infant doth." Then he went on to say in a soothing Tone, " There hath noe Misfortune hap-
" pened to us, but such as is common to
" the Lot of alle Men. We are alle
" Sinners, even to the youngest, fayrest,
" and seeminglie purest among us; and
" Death entered the World by Sin, and,
" constituted as we are, we would not,
" even if we could, dispense with Death.
" For, where doth it convey us? From
" this burthensome, miserable World, into
" the generall Assemblie of *Christ's* First-
" born, to be united with the Spiritts
" of the Just made perfect, to partake of
" everie Enjoyment which in this World
" is

"is unconnected with Sin, together with
"others that are unknowne and unspeak-
"able. And there, we shall agayn have
"*Bodies* as well as Soules; Eyes to see,
"but not to shed Tears; Voices to speak
"and sing, not to utter Lamentations;
"Hands, to doe *God's* Work; Feet, and
"it may be, Wings, to carry us on his
"Errands. Such will be the Blessedness
"of his glorified Saints; even of those
"who, having been Servants of Satan till
"the eleventh Hour, laboured penitentlie
"and diligentlie for their heavenlie Master
"one Hour before Sunset; but as for
"those who, dying in mere Infancie,
"never committed actual Sin, they follow
"the Lamb whithersoever he goeth!
"'Oh, think of this, dear *Rose*, and
"Sorrow not as those without Hope;
"for be assured, your Child hath more
"reall Reason to be grieved for you, than
"you for *him*.'"

With this, and like Discourse, that distilled like the Dew, or the small Rain on the tender Grasse, did *Roger Agnew* comfort

fort his Wife, untill the Moon had risen. Likewise he spake to us of those who lay buried arounde, how one had died of a broken Heart, another of suddain Joy, another had let Patience have her perfect Work through Years of lingering Disease. Then we walked slowlie and composedlie Home, and ate our Supper peacefullie, *Rose* not refusing to eat, though she took but little.

Since that Evening, she hath, at Mr. *Agnew's* Wish, gone much among the Poor, reading to one, working for another, carrying Food and Medicine to another; and in this I have borne her Companie. I like it well. Methinks how pleasant and seemlie are the Duties of a country Minister's Wife! a God-fearing Woman, that is, who considereth the Poor and Needy, insteade of aiming to be frounced and purfled like her richest Neighbours. Mr. *Agnew* was reading to us, last Night, of *Bernard Gilpin*—he of whom the *Lord Burleigh* sayd, "Who can blame that Man for
" not

"not accepting a Bishopric?" How charmed were we with the Description of the Simplicitie and Hospitalitie of his Method of living at *Houghton!*—There is another Place of nearlie the same Name, in *Buckinghamshire*—not *Houghton*, but *Horton*, . . . where one Mr. *John Milton* spent five of the best Years of his Life,—and where methinks his Wife could have been happier with him than in *St. Bride's Churchyarde*.—But it profits not to wish and to will.—What was to be, had Need to be, soe there's an End.

Aug. 1.

MR. *AGNEW* sayd to me this Morning, somewhat gravelie, "I observe, *Cousin*, "you seem to consider "yourselfe the Victim of "Circumstances." "And "am I not?" I replied. "No," he answered, "Circumstance is a false God, "unrecognised by the Christian, who "contemns

" contemns him, though a stubborn yet
" a profitable Servant."—"That may be
" alle very grand for a Man to doe," I
sayd. "Very grand, but very feasible,
" for a Woman as well as a Man," rejoined Mr. *Agnew*, "and we shall be
" driven to the Walle all our Lives, unless
" we have this victorious Struggle with
" Circumstances. I seldom allude, *Cousin*,
" to yours, which are almoste too deli-
" cate for me to meddle with; and yet
" I hardlie feele justified in letting soe
" many Opportunities escape. Do I
" offend? or may I go on? — Onlie
" think, then, how voluntarilie you have
" placed yourself in your present uncom-
" fortable Situation. The Tree cannot
" resist the graduall Growth of the Moss
" upon it; but you might, anie Day,
" anie Hour, have freed yourself from
" the equallie graduall Formation of the
" Net that has enclosed you at last. You
" entered too hastilie into your firste—
" nay, let that pass,—you gave too shorte
" a Triall of your new Home before you
                                   " became

"became disgusted with it. Admit it
"to have beene dull, even unhealthfulle,
"were you justified in forsaking it at a
"Month's End? But your Husband
"gave you Leave of Absence, though
"obtayned on false Pretences.— When
"you found them to be false, should
"you not have cleared yourself to him
"of Knowledge of the Deceit? Then
"your Leave, soe obtayned, expired—
"shoulde you not have returned then?
"—Your Health and Spiritts were re-
"cruited; your Husband wrote to reclaim
"you— shoulde you not have returned
"then? He provided an Escort, whom
"your Father beat and drove away.—
"If you had insisted on going to your
"Husband, might you not have gone
"*then?* Oh, *Cousin,* you dare not look
"up to Heaven and say you have been
"the Victim of Circumstances."

 I made no Answer; onlie felt much
moven, and very angrie. I sayd, "If
"I wished to goe back, Mr. *Milton*
"woulde not receive me now."

         "Will

"Will you try?" sayd *Roger*. "Will you but let me try? Will you let me write to him?"

I had a Mind to say "Yes."—Insteade, I answered "No."

"Then there's an End," cried he sharplie. "Had you made but one fayre Triall, whether successfulle or noe, I coulde have been satisfied—no, not satisfied, but I woulde have esteemed you, coulde have taken your Part. As it is, the less I say just now, perhaps, the better. Forgive me for having spoken at alle."

——Afterwards, I hearde him say to *Rose* of me, "I verilie believe there is Nothing in her on which to make a permanent Impression. I verilie think she loves everie one of those long Curls of hers more than she loves Mr. *Milton*."

(Note:—I will cut them two Inches shorter to-night. And they will grow all the faster.)

. . . Oh, my sad Heart, *Roger Agnew* hath pierced you at last!

I

I was moved, more than he thought, by what he had sayd in the Morning; and, in writing down the Heads of his Speech, to kill Time, a kind of Resentment at myselfe came over me, unlike to what I had ever felt before; in spite of my Folly about my Curls. Seeking for some Trifle in a Bag that had not been shaken out since I brought it from *London*, out tumbled a Key with curious Wards— I knew it at once for one that belonged to a certayn Algum-wood Casket Mr. *Milton* had Recourse to dailie, because he kept small Change in it; and I knew not I had brought it away! 'Twas worked in Grotesque, the Casket, by *Benvenuto*, for *Clement* the Seventh, who for some Reason woulde not have it; and soe it came somehow to *Clementillo*, who gave it to Mr. *Milton*. Thought I, how uncomfortable the Loss of this Key must have made him! he must have needed it a hundred Times! even if he hath bought a new Casket, I will for it he habituallie goes agayn and agayn to the old one, and then

then he remembers that he lost the Key the same Day that he lost his Wife. I heartilie wish he had it back. Ah, but he feels not the one Loss as he feels the other. Nay, but it is as well that one of them, tho' the Lesser, should be repaired. 'Twill shew Signe of Grace, my thinking of him, and may open the Way, if *God* wills, to some Interchange of Kindnesse, however fleeting.

Soe I soughte out Mr. *Agnew*, tapping at his Studdy Doore. He sayd, "Come "in," drylie enoughe; and there were he and *Rose* reading a Letter. I sayd, "I "want you to write for me to Mr. "*Milton*." He gave a sour Look, as much as to say he disliked the Office; which threw me back, as 'twere; he having soe lately proposed it himself. *Rose's* Eyes, however, dilated with sweete Pleasure, as she lookt from one to the other of us.

"Well,—I fear 'tis too late," sayd he at length reluctantlie, I mighte almost say grufflie,—" what am I to write?"

"To

"To tell him I have this Key," I made Answer faltering.

"That Key!" cried he.

"Yes, the Key of his Algum-wood "Casket, which I knew not I had, and "which I think he must miss dailie."

He lookt at me with the utmost Impatience. "And is that alle?" he sayd.

"Yes, alle," I sayd trembling.

"And have you nothing more to tell "him?" sayd he.

"No—" after a Pause, I replyed. *Rose's* Countenance fell.

"Then you must ask some one else "to write for you, Mrs. *Milton*," burste forthe *Roger Agnew*, "unless you choose "to write for yourself. I have neither "Part nor Lot in it."

I burste forthe into Teares.

—"No, *Rose*, no," repeated Mr. *Agnew*, putting aside his Wife, who woulde have interceded for me,—"her Teares have "noe Effect on me now—they proceed, "not from a contrite Heart, they are the "Tears of a Child that cannot brook to
"be

"be chidden for the Waywardnesse in
"which it persists."

"You doe me Wrong everie Way," I sayd; "I came to you willing and desi-
"rous to doe what you yourselfe woulde,
"this Morning, have had me doe."

"But in how strange a Way!" cried he. "At a Time when anie Renewal of
"your Intercourse requires to be con-
"ducted with the utmost Delicacy, and
"even with more Shew of Concession on
"your Part than, an Hour ago, I should
"have deemed needfulle,—to propose an
"abrupt, trivial Communication about an
"old Key!"

"It needed not to have been abrupt," I sayd, "nor yet trivial; for I meant it to
"have beene exprest kindlie."

"You said not that before," answered he.

"Because you gave me not Time.—Be-
"cause you chid me and frightened me."

He stood silent, some While, upon this; grave, yet softer, and mechanicallie playing with the Key, which he had taken from my Hand. *Rose* looking in his Face anxiouslie.

anxiouslie. At lengthe, to disturbe his Reverie, she playfulle tooke it from him, saying, in School-girl Phrase,

"This is the Key of the Kingdom!"

"Of the Kingdom of Heaven, it mighte
" be!" exclaimed *Roger*, "if we knew
" how to use it arighte! If we knew but
" how to fit it to the Wards of *Milton's*
" Heart!—there's the Difficultie . . . a
" greater one, poor *Moll*, than you know;
" for hithertoe, alle the Reluctance has
" been on your Part. But now . . ."

"What now?" I anxiouslie askt.

"We were talking of you but as you rejoyned us," sayd Mr. *Agnew*, "and I
" was telling *Rose* that hithertoe I had
" considered the onlie Obstacle to a Re-
" union arose from a false Impression of
" your own, that Mr. *Milton* coulde not
" make you happy. But now I have
" beene led to the Conclusion that you
" cannot make *him* soe, which increases
" the Difficultie."

After a Pause, I sayd, "What makes
" you think soe?"

"You

"You and he have made me think soe," he replyed. "First for yourself, dear "*Moll*, putting aside for a Time the "Consideration of your Youth, Beauty, "Franknesse, Mirthfullenesse, and a cer- "tayn girlish Drollerie and Mischiefe "that are all very well in fitting Time "and Place,—what remains in you for "a Mind like *John Milton's* to repose "upon? what Stabilitie? what Sym- "pathie? what steadfast Principle? You "take noe Pains to apprehend and relish "his favourite Pursuits; you care not "for his wounded Feelings, you consult "not his Interests, anie more than your "owne Duty. Now, is such the Char- "acter to make *Milton* happy?"

"No one can answer that but himself," I replyed, deeplie mortyfide.

"Well, he *has* answered it," sayd Mr. *Agnew*, taking up the Letter he and *Rose* had beene reading when I interrupted them. . . . "You must know, *Cousin*, "that his and my close Friendship hath "beene a good deal interrupted by this "Matter.

"Matter. 'Twas under my Roof you
" met. *Rose* had imparted to me much
" of her earlie Interest in you. I fancied
" you had good Dispositions which, under
" masterlie Trayning, would ripen into
" noble Principles; and therefore pro-
" moted your Marriage as far as my
" Interest with your Father had Weight.
" I own I was surprised at his easilie
" obtayned Consent. . . . but, that *you*,
" once domesticated with such a Man
" as *John Milton*, shoulde find your
" Home uninteresting, your Affections
" free to stray back to your owne Family,
" was what I had never contemplated."

Here I made a Show of taking the Letter, but he held it back.

" No, *Moll*, you disappointed us everie
" Way. And, for a time, *Rose* and I
" were ashamed, *for* you rather than of
" you, that we left noe Means neglected
" of trying to preserve your Place in
" your Husband's Regard. But you did
" not bear us out; and then he beganne
" to take it amisse that we upheld you.
"Soe

"Soe then, after some warm and cool Words, our Correspondence languished; and hath but now beene renewed."

"He has written us a most kind Condolence," interrupted *Rose*, "on the Death of our Baby."

"Yes, most kindlie, most nobly exprest," sayd Mr. *Agnew*; "but what a Conclusion!"

And then, after this long Preamble, he offered me the Letter, the Beginning of which, tho' doubtlesse well enough, I marked not, being impatient to reach the latter Part; wherein I found myself spoken of soe bitterlie, soe harshlie, as that I too plainly saw *Roger Agnew* had not beene beside the Mark when he decided I could never make Mr. *Milton* happy. Payned and wounded Feeling made me lay aside the Letter without proffering another Word, and retreat without soe much as a Sigh or a Sob into mine own Chamber; but noe longer could the Restraynt be maintained. I fell to weeping soe passionatelie that *Rose* prayed

prayed to come in, and condoled with me, and advised me, soe as that at length my weeping bated, and I promised to return below when I shoulde have bathed mine Eyes and smoothed my Hair; but I have not gone down yet.

Bedtime.

THINK I shall send to *Father* to have me home at the Beginning of next Week. *Rose* needes me not, now; and it cannot be pleasant to Mr. *Agnew* to see my sorrowfulle Face about the House. His Reproofe and my Husband's together have riven my Heart; I think I shall never laugh agayn, nor smile but after a piteous Sorte; and soe People will cease to love me, for there is Nothing in me of a graver Kind to draw their Affection; and soe I shall lead a moping Life unto the End of my Dayes.

—Luckilie for me, *Rose* hath much Sewing to doe; for she hath undertaken
with

with great Energie her Labours for the
Poore, and consequentlie spends less Time
in her Husband's Studdy; and, as I help
her to the best of my Means, my Sewing hides my Lack of Talking, and Mr.
Agnew reads to us such Books as he deems
entertayning; yet, half the Time, I hear
not what he reads. Still, I did not deeme
so much Amusement could have beene
found in Books; and there are some of
his, that, if not soe cumbrous, I woulde
fain borrow.

Friday.

HAVE made up my Mind
now, that I shall never see
Mr. *Milton* more; and am
resolved to submitt to it
without another Tear.

Rose sayd, this Morning,
she was glad to see me more composed;
and soe am I; but never was more
miserable.

Saturday

Saturday Night.

MR. *AGNEW'S* religious Services at the End of the Week have alwaies more than usuall Matter and Meaninge in them. They are neither soe drowsy as those I have beene for manie Years accustomed to at Home, nor soe wearisome as to remind me of the *Puritans.* Were there manie such as he in our Church, soe faithfulle, fervent, and thoughtfulle, methinks there would be fewer Schismaticks; but still there woulde be some, because there are alwaies some that like to be the uppermost.... To-nighte, Mr. *Agnew's* Prayers went straight to my Heart; and I privilie turned sundrie of his generall Petitions into particular ones, for myself and *Robin,* and also for Mr. *Milton.* This gave such unwonted Relief, that since I entered into my Closet, I have repeated the same particularlie; one Request seeming to grow out of another, till I remained I know not

not how long on my Knees, and will bend them yet agayn, ere I go to Bed.

How sweetlie the Moon shines through my Casement to-night! I am almoste avised to accede to *Rose's* Request of staying here to the End of the Month :— everie Thing here is soe peacefulle ; and *Forest Hill* is dull, now *Robin* is away.

Sunday Evening.

HOW blessed a Sabbath !— Can it be, that I thought, onlie two Days back, I shoulde never know Peace agayn? Joy I may not, but Peace I can and doe. And yet nought hath amended the unfortunate Condition of mine Affairs ; but a different Colouring is caste upon them —the *Lord* grant that it may last ! How hath it come soe, and how may it be preserved? This Morn, when I awoke, 'twas with a Sense of Relief such as we have when we miss some wearying bodilie Payn ; a Feeling as though I had beene forgiven,

forgiven, yet not by Mr. *Milton*, for I knew he had not forgiven me. Then, it must be, I was forgiven by *God;* and why? I had done nothing to get his Forgivenesse, only presumed on his Mercy to ask manie Things I had noe Right to expect. And yet I felt I *was* forgiven. Why then mighte not Mr. *Milton* some Day forgive me? Should the Debt of ten thousand Talents be cancelled, and not the Debt of a hundred Pence? Then I thought on that same Word, Talents; and considered, had I ten, or even one? Decided to consider it at leisure, more closelie, and to make over to *God* henceforthe, be they ten, or be it one. Then, dressed with much Composure, and went down to Breakfast.

Having marked that Mr. *Agnew* and *Rose* affected not Companie on this Day, spent it chieflie by myself, except at Church and Meal-times; partlie in my Chamber, partlie in the Garden Bowre by the Bee-hives. Made manie Resolutions, which, in Church, I converted

verted into Prayers and Promises. Hence, my holy Peace.

Monday.

ROSE proposed, this Morning, we shoulde resume our Studdies. Felt loath to comply, but did soe neverthelesse, and afterwards we walked manie Miles, to visit some poor Folk. This Evening, Mr. *Agnew* read us the Prologue to the *Canterbury Tales*. How lifelike are the Portraitures! I mind me that Mr. *Milton* shewed me the *Talbot* Inn, that Day we crost the River with Mr. *Marvell*.

Tuesday.

HOW heartilie do I wish I had never read that same Letter!—or rather, that it had never beene written. Thus it is, even with our Wishes. We think ourselves reasonable in wishing some small Thing

Thing were otherwise, which it were quite as impossible to alter as some great Thing. Neverthelesse I cannot help fretting over the Remembrance of that Part wherein he spake such bitter Things of my "most ungoverned Passion for "Revellings and Junketings." Sure, he would not call my Life too merrie now, could he see me lying wakefulle on my Bed, could he see me preventing the Morning Watch, could he see me at my Prayers, at my Books, at my Needle. . . . He shall find he hath judged too hardlie of poor *Moll*, even yet.

Wednesday.

TOOK a cold Dinner in a Basket with us to-day, and ate our rusticall Repast on the Skirt of a Wood, where we could see the Squirrels at theire Gambols. Mr. *Agnew* lay on the Grasse, and *Rose* took out her knitting, whereat he laught, and sayd she was like the *Dutch* Women,

Women, that must knit, whether mourning or feasting, and even on the Sabbath. Having laught her out of her Work, he drew forth Mr. *George Herbert's* Poems, and read us a Strayn which pleased *Rose* and me soe much, that I shall copy it herein, to have always by me.

*How fresh, oh Lord; how sweet and clean
Are thy Returns! e'en as the Flowers in Spring,
To which, beside theire owne Demesne,
The late pent Frosts Tributes of Pleasure bring.
Grief melts away like Snow in May,
As if there were noe such cold Thing.*

*Who would have thought my shrivelled Heart
Woulde have recovered greenness? it was gone
Quite Underground, as Flowers depart
To see their Mother-root, when they have blown,
Where they together, alle the hard Weather,
Dead to the World, keep House alone.*

*These are thy Wonders, Lord of Power!
Killing and quickening, bringing down to Hell
And up to Heaven, in an Hour,
Making a Chiming of a passing Bell.
We say amiss "this or that is;"
Thy Word is alle, if we could spell.*

Oh that I once past changing were!
Fast in thy Paradise, where no Flowers can wither;
Manie a Spring I shoot up faire,
Offering at Heaven, growing and groaning thither,
Nor doth my Flower want a Spring Shower,
My Sins and I joyning together.

But while I grow in a straight Line,
Still upwards bent, as if Heaven were my own,
Thy Anger comes, and I decline.—
What Frost to that? What Pole is not the Zone
Where alle Things burn, when thou dost turn,
And the least Frown of thine is shewn?

And now, in Age, I bud agayn,
After soe manie Deaths, I bud and write,
I once more smell the Dew and Rain,
And relish Versing! Oh my onlie Light!
It cannot be that I am he
On whom thy Tempests fell alle Night?

These are thy Wonders, Lord of Love,
To make us see we are but Flowers that glide,
Which, when we once can feel and prove,
Thou hast a Garden for us where to bide.
Who would be more, swelling their Store,
Forfeit their Paradise by their Pride.

Thursday.

Thursday.

FATHER sent over *Diggory* with a Letter for me from deare *Robin:* alsoe, to ask when I was minded to return Home, as *Mother* wants to goe to *Sandford.* Fixed the Week after next; but *Rose* says I must be here agayn at the Applegathering. Answered *Robin's* Letter. He looketh not for Choyce of fine Words; nor noteth an Error here and there in the Spelling.

Tuesday.

LIFE flows away here in such unmarked Tranquilitie, that one hath Nothing whereof to write, or to remember what distinguished one Day from another. I am sad, yet not dulle; methinks I have grown some Yeares older since I came here. I can fancy elder Women feeling much

much as I doe now. I have Nothing to desire, Nothing to hope, that is likelie to come to pass—Nothing to regret, except I begin soe far back, that my whole Life hath neede, as 'twere, to begin over agayn. . . .

Mr. *Agnew* translates to us Portions of *Thuanus* his Historie, and the Letters of *Theodore Beza*, concerning the *French* Reformed Church; oft prolix, yet interesting, especially with Mr. *Agnew's* Comments, and Allusions to our own Time. On the other Hand, *Rose* reads *Davila*, the sworne Apologiste of *Catherine de' Medicis*, whose charming *Italian* even I can comprehende; but alle is false and plausible. How sad, that the wrong Partie shoulde be victorious! Soe it may befall in this Land; though, indeede, I have hearde soe much bitter Rayling on bothe Sides, that I know not which is right. The Line of Demarcation is not soe distinctly drawn, methinks, as 'twas in *France*. Yet it cannot be right to take up Arms agaynst constituted Authorities? Yet,

Yet, and if those same Authorities abuse their Trust? Nay, Women cannot understand these Matters, and I thank Heaven they need not. Onlie, they cannot help siding with those they love; and sometimes those they love are on opposite sides.

Mr. *Agnew* sayth, the secular Arm shoulde never be employed in spirituall Matters, and that the *Hugenots* committed a grave Mistake in choosing Princes and Admirals for their Leaders, insteade of simple Preachers with Bible in their Hands; and he askt, " did *Luther* or *Peter* " the Hermit most manifestlie labour " with the Blessing of *God?*"

. . . I have noted the Heads of Mr. *Agnew's* Readings, after a Fashion of *Rose's*, in order to have a shorte, comprehensive Account of the Whole; and this hath abridged my journalling. It is the more profitable to me of the two, changes the sad Current of Thought, and, though an unaccustomed Task, I like it well.

Saturday.

Saturday.

ON *Monday* I return to *Forest Hill.* I am well pleased to have yet another *Sheepscote* Sabbath. To-day we had the rare Event of a Dinner-guest; soe full of what the Rebels are doing, and alle the

Horrors of Strife, that he seemed to us quiete Folks, like the Denizen of another World.

Forest

Forest Hill, August 3.

HOME agayn, and *Mother* hath gone on her long intended Visitt to Uncle *John*, taking with her the two youngest. *Father* much preoccupide, by reason of the Supplies needed for his Majesty's Service; soe that, sweet *Robin* being away, I find myselfe lonely. *Harry* rides with me in the Evening, but the Mornings I have alle to myself; and when I have fulfilled *Mother's* Behests in the Kitchen and Still-room, I have nought but to read in our somewhat scant Collection of Books, the moste Part whereof are religious. And (not on that Account, but by reason I have read the most of them before), methinks I will write to borrow some of *Rose*; for Change of Reading hath now become a Want. I am minded also, to seek out and minister unto some poore Folk after her Fashion. Now that I am Queen of the

the Larder, there is manie a wholesome Scrap at my Disposal, and there are likewise sundrie Physiques in my Mother's Closet, which she addeth to Year by Year, and never wants, we are soe seldom ill.

Aug. 5.

DEAR *Father* sayd this Evening, as we came in from a Walk on the Terrace, "My sweet *Moll*, you "were ever the Light of "the House; but now, "though you are more staid than of "former Time, I find you a better Com- "panion than ever. This last Visitt to "*Sheepscote* hath evened your Spiritts."

Poor *Father!* he knew not how I lay awake and wept last Night, for one I shall never see agayn, nor how the Terrace Walk minded me of him. My Spiritts may seem even, and I exert myself to please; but, within, all is dark Shade, or at best, grey Twilight; and my my Spiritts are, in Fact, worse here than they were at *Sheepscote*, because, here, I am continuallie thinking of one whose Name is never uttered; whereas, there, it was mentioned naturallie and tenderlie, though sadly. . . .

I will forthe to see some of the poor Folk.

Same Night.

RESOLVED to make the Circuit of the Cottages, but onlie reached the first, wherein I found poor *Nell* in such Grief of Body and Mind, that I was avised to wait with her a long Time. Askt why she had not sent to us for Relief; was answered she had thought of doing soe, but was feared of making too free. After a lengthened Visitt, which seemed to relieve her Mind, and certaynlie relieved mine, I bade her Farewell, and at the Wicket met my Father coming up with a playn-favoured but scholarlike looking reverend

reverend Man. He sayd, "*Moll*, I could not think what had become of you." I answered, I hoped I had not kept him waiting for Dinner—poor *Nell* had entertayned me longer than I wisht, with the Catalogue of her Troubles. The Stranger looking attentively at me, observed that may be the poor Woman had entertayned an Angel unawares ; and added, "Doubt not, Madam, we woulde rather await our Dinner than that you should have curtayled your Message of Charity." Hithertoe, my Father had not named this Gentleman to me ; but now he sayd, "Child, this is the Reverend Doctor *Jeremy Taylor*, Chaplain in Ordinarie to his Majesty, and whom you know I have heard more than once preach before the King since he abode in *Oxford*." Thereon I made a lowly Reverence, and we walked homewards together. At first, he discoursed chiefly with my Father on the Troubles of the Times, and then he drew me into the Dialogue, in the Course of which I let fall a Saying of Mr. *Agnew's*

Agnew's which drew from the reverend Gentleman a respectfulle Look I felt I no Way deserved. Soe then I had to explain that the Saying was none of mine, and felt ashamed he shoulde suppose me wiser than I was, especiallie as he commended my Modesty. But we progressed well, and he soon had the Discourse all to himself, for Squire *Paice* came up, and detained *Father*, while the Doctor and I walked on. I could not help reflecting how odd it was, that I, whom Nature had endowed with such a very ordinarie Capacitie, and scarce anie Taste for Letters, shoulde continuallie be thrown into the Companie of the cleverest of Men,—first, Mr. *Milton;* then Mr. *Agnew;* and now, this Doctor *Jeremy Taylor.* But, like the other two, he is not merely clever, he is Christian and good. How much I learnt in this short Interview! for short it seemed, though it must have extended over a good half Hour. He sayd, " Perhaps, young Lady, the Time " may come when you shall find safer
" Solace

"Solace in the Exercise of the Charities
"than of the Affections. Safer: for, not
"to consider how a successfulle or unsuc-
"cessfulle Passion for a human Being of
"like Infirmities with ourselves, oft stains
"and darkens and shortens the Current
"of Life, even the chastened Love of a
"Mother for her Child, as of *Octavia*,
"who swooned at '*Tu, Marcellus, eris*,'
"—or of Wives for their Husbands,
"as *Artemisia* and *Laodamia*, sometimes
"amounting to Idolatry—nay, the Love
"of Friend for Friend, while alle is sweet
"Influences and animating Transports, yet
"exceeding the Reasonableness of that of
"*David* for *Jonathan*, or of our blessed
"*Lord* for *St. John* and the Family of
"*Lazarus*, may procure far more Tor-
"ment than Profit: even if the Attach-
"ment is reciprocal, and well grounded,
"and equallie matcht, which often it is
"not. Then interpose human Tempers,
"and Chills, and Heates, and Slyghtes
"fancied or intended, which make the
"vext Soul readie to wish it had never
"existed.

"existed. How smalle a Thing is a
"human Heart! you might grasp it in
"your little Hand; and yet its Strifes
"and Agonies are enough to distend a
"Skin that should cover the whole
"World! But, in the Charities, what
"Peace! yea, they distill Sweetnesse
"even from the Unthankfulle, blessing
"him that gives more than him that
"receives; while, in the Main, they are
"laid out at better Interest than our
"warmest Affections, and bring in a far
"richer Harvest of Love and Gratitude.
"Yet, let our Affections have their fitting
"Exercise too, staying ourselves with the
"Reflection, that there is greater Happi-
"nesse, after alle Things sayd, in loving
"than in being loved, save by the *God* of
"Love who first loved us, and that they
"who dwell in Love dwell in *Him*."

Then he went on to speak of the manifold Acts and Divisions of Charity; as much, methought, in the Vein of a Poet as a Preacher; and he minded me much of that Scene in the tenth Book of the
Fairie

Fairie Queene, soe lately read to us by Mr. *Agnew*, wherein the *Red Cross Knight* and *Una* were shown *Mercy* at her work.

Aug. 10.

A PACK-HORSE from *Sheepscote* just reported, laden with a goodlie Store of Books, besides sundrie smaller Tokens of *Rose's* thoughtfulle Kindnesse. I have now methodicallie divided my Time into stated Hours, of Prayer, Exercise, Studdy, Housewiferie, and Acts of Mercy, on however a humble Scale; and find mine owne Peace of Mind thereby increased notwithstanding the Darknesse of publick and Dullnesse of private Affairs.

Made out the Meaning of "Cynosure" and "Cimmerian Darknesse." . . .

Aug.

Aug. 15.

FULL sad am I to learn that Mr. *Milton* hath published another book in Advocacy of Divorce. Alas, why will he chafe against the Chain, and widen the cruel Division between us? My Father is outrageous on the Matter, and speaks soe passionatelie of him, that it is worse than not speaking of him at alle, which latelie I was avised to complain of.

Aug. 30.

DICK beginneth to fancie himself in Love with *Audrey Paice*—an Attachment that will doe him noe good: his Tastes alreadie want raising, and she will onlie lower them, I feare,—a comely, romping, noisie Girl, that, were she but a Farmer's Daughter, woulde be the Life and Soul of alle the Whitsun-ales,

ales, Harvest-homes, and Hay-makings in the Country: in short, as fond of idling and merrymaking as I once was myself: onlie I never was soe riotous.

I beginne to see Faults in *Dick* and *Harry* I never saw before. Is my Taste bettering, or my Temper worsenning? At alle Events, we have noe cross Words, for I expect them not to alter, knowing how hard it is to doe soe by myself.

I look forward with Pleasure to my *Sheepscote* Visitt. Dear *Mother* returneth to-morrow. Good Dr. *Taylor* hath twice taken the Trouble to walk over from *Oxford* to see me, but he hath now left, and we may never meet agayn. His Visitts have beene very precious to me: I think he hath some Glimmering of my sad Case: indeed, who knows it not? At parting he sayd, smiling, he hoped he should yet hear of my making Offerings to *Viriplaca* on *Mount Palatine;* then added, gravelie, "You know where reall "Offerings may be made and alwaies "accepted—Offerings of spare Half-hours
"and

" and Five-minutes, when we shut the
" Closet Door and commune with our
" own Hearts and are still." Alsoe he
sayd, "There are Sacrifices to make which
" sometimes wring our very Hearts to
" offer; but our gracious God accepts
" them neverthelesse, if our Feet be really
" in the right Path, even though, like
" *Chryseis*, we look back, weeping."

He sayd . . . But how manie Things as beautifulle and true did I hear my Husband say, which passed by me like the idle Wind that I regarded not!

Sept. 8.

HARRY hath just broughte in the News of his Majesty's Success in the West. Lord *Essex's* Army hath beene completely surrounded by the royal Troops; himself forct to escape in a boat to *Plymouth*, and all the Arms, Artillerie, Baggage, &c., of *Skippon's* Men have fallen into the Hands of of the King. *Father* is soe pleased that he hath mounted the Flag, and given double Allowance of Ale to his Men.

I wearie to hear from *Robin*.

Sheepscote, Oct. 10.

HOW sweete a Picture of rurall Life did *Sheepscote* present, when I arrived here this Afternoon! The Water being now much out, the Face of the Countrie presented a new Aspect: there were men threshing the Walnut Trees, Children and Women putting the Nuts into Osier Baskets, a Bailiff on a white Horse overlooking them, and now and then galloping to another Party, and splashing through the Water. Then we found Mr. *Agnew* equallie busie with his Apples, mounted half Way up one of the Trees, and throwing Cherry Pippins down into *Rose's* Apron, and now and then making as though he would pelt her:
onlie

onlie she dared him, and woulde not be frightened. Her Donkey, chewing Apples in the Corner, with the Cider running out of his Mouth, presented a ludicrous Image of Enjoyment, and 'twas evidently enhanct by *Giles*' brushing his rough Coat with a Birch Besom, instead of minding his owne Businesse of sweeping the Walk. The Sun, shining with mellow Light on the mown Grass and fresh clipt Hornbeam Hedges, made even the commonest Objects distinct and cheerfulle; and the Air was soe cleare, we coulde hear the Village Children afar off at theire Play.

Rose had abundance of delicious new Honey in the Comb, and Bread hot from the Oven, for our earlie Supper. *Dick* was tempted to stay too late; however, he is oft as late, now, returning from *Audrey Paice*, though my Mother likes it not.

Oct.

Oct. 15.

OSE is quite in good Spiritts now, and we go on most harmoniouslie and happilie. Alle our Tastes are now in common; and I never more enjoyed this Union of Seclusion and Society. Besides, Mr. *Agnew* is more than commonlie kind, and never speaks sternlie or sharplie to me now. Indeed, this Morning, looking thoughtfullie at me, he sayd, "I know "not, *Cousin*, what Change has come over "you, but you are now alle that a wise "Man coulde love and approve." I sayd, It must be owing then to Dr. *Jeremy Taylor*, who had done me more goode, it woulde seeme, in three Lessons, than he or Mr. *Milton* coulde imparte in thirty or three hundred. He sayd he was inclined to attribute it to a higher Source than that; and yet, there was doubtlesse a great Knack in teaching, and there was

a

a good deal in liking the Teacher. He had alwaies hearde the Doctor spoken of as a good, pious, and clever Man, though rather too high a Prelatist. I sayd, "There were good Men of alle Sorts: "there was Mr. *Milton*, who woulde "pull the Church down; there was "Mr. *Agnew*, who woulde only have it "mended; and there was Dr. *Jeremy* "*Taylor*, who was content with it as it "stoode." Then *Rose* askt me of the puritanicall Preachers. Then I showed her how they preached, and made her laugh. But Mr. *Agnew* woulde not laugh. But I made him laugh at last. Then he was angrie with himself and with me; only not very angry; and sayd, I had a Right to a Name which he knew had been given me, of "cleaving Mischief." I knew not he knew of it, and was checked, though I laught it off.

Oct.

Oct. 16.

WALKING together, this Morning, *Rose* was avised to say, "Did Mr. *Milton* "ever tell you the Adven- "tures of the *Italian* Lady?" "Rely on it he never did," said Mr. *Agnew.*—"*Milton* is as modest a "Man as ever breathed—alle Men of first "class Genius are soe." "What was the "Adventure?" I askt, curiouslie. "Why, "I neede not tell you, *Moll*, that *John* "*Milton*, as a Youth, was extremelie "handsome, even beautifull. His Colour "came and went soe like a Girl's, that "we of *Christ's* College used to call him "'the Lady,' and thereby annoy him noe "little. One summer Afternoone he and "I and young *King* (*Lycidas*, you know) "had started on a country Walk, (the "Countrie is not pretty, round *Cambridge*) "when we met in with an Acquaintance "whom Mr. *Milton* affected not, soe he "sayd he would walk on to the first rising "Ground

they paused in surprise at seeing "Milton asleep"

" Ground and wait us there. On this
" rising Ground stood a Tree, beneath
" which our impatient young Gentleman
" presentlie cast himself, and, having
" walked fast, and the Weather being
" warm, soon falls asleep as sound as a
" Top. Meantime, *King* and I quit our
" Friend and saunter forward pretty easilie.
" Anon comes up with us a Caroche, with
" something I know not what of out-
" landish in its Build; and within it, two
" Ladies, one of them having the fayrest
" Face I ever set Eyes on, present Com-
" panie duly excepted. The Caroche
" having passed us, *King* and I mutuallie
" express our Admiration, and thereupon,
" preferring Turf to Dust, got on the
" other Side the Hedge, which was not
" soe thick but that we could make out
" the Caroche, and see the Ladies descend
" from it, to walk up the Hill. Having
" reached the Tree, they paused in Sur-
" prise at seeing *Milton* asleep beneath it;
" and in prettie dumb Shew, which we
" watcht sharplie, exprest their Admira-
           " tion

"tion of his Appearance and Posture,
"which woulde have suited an *Arcadian*
"well enough. The younger Lady, has-
"tilie taking out a Pencil and Paper,
"wrote something which she laughinglie
"shewed her Companion, and then put
"into the Sleeper's Hand. Thereupon,
"they got into their Caroche, and drove
"off. *King* and I, dying with Curiositie
"to know what she had writ, soon roused
"our Friend and possest ourselves of the
"Secret. The Verses ran thus . . .

> *Occhi, Stelle mortali,*
> *Ministre de miei Mali,*
> *Se, chiusi, m' uccidete,*
> *Aperti, che farete?*

"*Milton* coloured, crumpled them up,
"and yet put them in his Pocket; then
"askt us what the Lady was like. And
"herein lay the Pleasantry of the Affair;
"for I truly told him she had a Pear-
"shaped Face, lustrous black Eyes, and
"a Skin that shewed '*il bruno il bel non*
"*toglie;*' whereas, *King*, in his Mischief,
"drew a fancy Portrait, much liker you,
"*Moll*,

"*Moll*, than the Incognita, which hit
"*Milton's* Taste soe much better, that he
"was believed for his Payns; and then
"he declared that I had beene describing
"the Duenna! . . . Some Time after,
"when *Milton* beganne to talk of visiting
"*Italy*, we bantered him, and sayd he
"was going to look for the Incognita.
"He stoode it well, and sayd, 'Laugh
"on! do you think I mind you? Not
"a Bit.' I think he did."

Just at this Turn, Mr. *Agnew* stumbled at something in the long Grass. It proved to be an old, rustie Horse-pistol. His Countenance changed at once from gay to grave. "I thought we had noe such "Things hereabouts yet," cried he, viewing it askance.—"I suppose I mighte as "well think I had found a Corner of "the Land where there was noe originall "Sin." And soe, flung it over the Hedge.

——First class Geniuses are always modest, are they?—Then I should say that young *Italian* Lady's Genius was not of the first Class.

Oct.

Oct. 19.

SPEAKING, to-day, of Mr. *Waller,* whom I had once seen at Uncle *John's,* Mr. *Agnew* sayd he had obtayned the Reputation of being one of our smoothest Versers, and thereupon brought forth one or two of his small pieces in Manuscript, which he read to *Rose* and me. They were addrest to the Lady *Dorothy Sydney;* and certainlie for specious Flatterie I doe not suppose they can be matcht; but there is noe Impress of reall Feeling in them. How diverse from my Husband's Versing! He never writ anie mere Love-verses, indeede, soe far as I know; but how much truer a Sence he hath of what is reallie beautifulle and becoming in a Woman than Mr. *Waller!* The Lady *Alice Egerton* mighte have beene more justlie proud of the fine Things written for her in *Comus,* than the Lady *Dorothea*
of

of anie of the fine Things written *of* her by this courtier-like Poet. For, to say that Trees bend down in homage to a Woman when she walks under them, and that the healing Waters of *Tonbridge* were placed there by Nature to compensate for the fatal Pride of *Sacharissa*, is soe fullesome and untrue as noe Woman, not devoured by Conceite, coulde endure; whereas, the Check that Villanie is sensible of in the Presence of Virtue, is most nobly, not extravagantlie, exprest by *Comus*. And though my Husband be almost too lavish, even in his short Pieces, of classic Allusion and Personation, yet, like antique Statues and Busts well placed in some statelie Pleasaunce, they are alwaies appropriate and gracefulle, which is more than can be sayd of Mr. *Waller's* overstrayned Figures and Metaphors.

Oct.

Oct. 20.

NEWS from Home: alle well. *Audrey Paice* on a Visitt there. I hope *Mother* hath not put her into my Chamber, but I know that she hath sett so manie Trays full of Spearmint, Peppermint, Camomiles, and Poppie-heads in the blue Chamber to dry, that she will not care to move them, nor have the Window opened lest they shoulde be blown aboute. I wish I had turned the Key on my ebony Cabinett.

Oct. 24.

RICHARD and *Audrey* rode over here, and spent a noisie Afternoone. *Rose* had the Goose dressed which I know she meant to have reserved for to-morrow. *Clover* was in a Heat, which one

one would have thoughte he needed not to have beene, with carrying a Lady; but *Audrey* is heavie. She treats *Dick* like a Boy; and, indeede, he is not much more; but he is quite taken up with her. I find she lies in the blue Chamber, which she says smells rarelie of Herbs. They returned not till late, after sundrie Hints from Mr. *Agnew*.

Oct. 27.

ALAS, alas, *Robin's* Silence is too sorrowfullie explained! He hath beene sent Home soe ill that he is like to die. This Report I have from *Diggory*, just come over to fetch me, with whom I start, soe soone as his Horse is bated. *Lord*, have Mercie on *Robin*.

The Children are alle sent away to keep the House quiete.

*At Robin's Bedside,
Saturday Night.*

OH, woefulle Sight! I had not known that pale Face, had I met it unawares. So thin and wan,—and he hath shot up into a tall Stripling during the last few Months. These two Nights of Watching have tried me sorelie, but I would not be witholden from sitting up with him yet agayn—what and if this Night should be his last? how coulde I forgive myself for sleeping on now and taking my Rest? The first Night, he knew me not; yet it was bitter-sweet to hear him chiding at sweet *Moll* for not coming. Yesternight he knew me for a While, kissed me, and fell into an heavie Sleepe, with his Hand locked in mine. We hoped the Crisis was come; but 'twas not soe. He raved much of a Man alle in red, riding hard after him. I minded me of those words, "the Enemy " sayd,

" sayd, I will overtake, I will pursue,"—and, noe one being by, save the unconscious Sufferer, I kneeled down beside him, and most earnestlie prayed for his Deliverance from all spirituall Adversaries. When I lookt up, his Eyes, larger and darker than ever, were fixt on me with a strange, wistfulle Stare, but he spake not. From that Moment he was quiete.

The Doctor thought him rambling this Morning, though I knew he was not, when he spake of an Angel in a long white Garment watching over him and kneeling by him in the Night.

Sunday Evening.

POOR *Nell* sitteth up with *Mother* to-night — right thankfulle is she to find that she can be of anie use: she says it seems soe strange that she should be able to make any Return for my Kindnesse. I must sleep to-night, that I may watch

watch to-morrow. The Servants are nigh spent, and are besides foolishlie afrayd of Infection. I hope *Rose* prays for me. Soe drowsie and dulle am I, as scarce to be able to pray for myself.

Monday.

OSE and Mr. *Agnew* come to abide with us for some Days. How thankfulle am I! Tears have relieved me.

Robin worse to-day. *Father* quite subdued. Mr. *Agnew* will sit up to-night, and insists on my sleeping.

Crab howled under my Window Yesternight as he did before my Wedding. I hope there is nothing in it. *Harry* got up and beat him, and at last put him in the Stable.

Tuesday.

Tuesday.

AFTER two Nights' Rest, I feel quite strengthened and restored this Morning. Deare *Rose* read me to sleep in her low, gentle Voice, and then lay down by my Side, twice stepping into *Robin's* Chamber during the Night, and bringing me News that all was well. Relieved in Mind, I slept heavilie nor woke till late. Then, returned to the sick Chamber, and found *Rose* bathing dear *Robin's* Temples with Vinegar, and changing his Pillow—his thin Hand rested on Mr. *Agnew*, on whom he lookt with a composed, collected Gaze. Slowlie turned his Eyes on me, and faintlie smiled, but spake not.

Poor dear *Mother* is ailing now. I sate with her and *Father* some Time; but it was a true Relief when *Rose* took my Place and let me return to the sick Room. *Rose* hath alreadie made several little Changes for the better; improved the

the Ventilation of *Robin's* Chamber, and prevented his hearing soe manie Noises. Alsoe, showed me how to make a pleasant cooling Drink, which he likes better than the warm Liquids, and which she assures me he may take with perfect Safetie.

Same Evening.

ROBIN vext, even to Tears, because the Doctor forbids the use of his cooling Drink, though it hath certainlie abated the Fever. At his Wish I stept down to intercede with the Doctor, then closetted with my Father, to discourse, as I suppose, of *Robin's* Symptoms. Insteade of which, found them earnestlie engaged on the never-ending Topick of Cavaliers and Roundheads. I was chafed and cut to the Heart, yet what can poor *Father* do; he is useless in the Sickroom, he is wearie of Suspense, and 'tis well if publick Affairs can divert him for an odd Half-hour.

The

The Doctor would not hear of *Robin* taking the cooling Beverage, and warned me that his Death woulde be upon my Head if I permitted him to be chilled: soe what could I doe? Poor *Robin* very impatient in consequence; and raving towards Midnight. *Rose* insisted in taking the last Half of my Watch.

I know not that I was ever more sorelie exercised than during the first Half of this Night. *Robin*, in his crazie Fit, would leave his Bed, and was soe strong as nearlie to master *Nell* and me, and I feared I must have called *Richard*. The next Minute he fell back as weak as a Child: we covered him up warm, and he was overtaken either with Stupor or Sleep. Earnestlie did I pray it might be the latter, and conduce to his healing. Afterwards, there being writing Implements at Hand, I wrote a Letter to Mr. *Milton*, which, though the Fancy of sending it soon died away, yet eased my Mind. When not in Prayer, I often find myself silently talking to him.

Wednesday.

Wednesday.

WAKING late after my scant Night's Rest, I found my Breakfaste neatlie layd out in the little Antechamber, to prevent the Fatigue of going down Stairs. A Handfulle of Autumn Flowers beside my Plate, left me in noe Doubt it was *Rose's* doing; and Mr. *Agnew* writing at the Window, told me he had persuaded my Father to goe to *Shotover* with *Dick.* Then laying aside his Pen, stept into the Sick-chamber for the latest News, which was good: and, sitting next me, talked of the Progress of *Robin's* Illnesse in a grave yet hopefulle Manner; leading, as he chieflie does, to high and unearthlie Sources of Consolation. He advised me to take a Turn in the fresh Ayr, though but as far as the two Junipers, before I entered *Robin's* Chamber, which, somewhat reluctantlie, I did; but the bright Daylight and warm Sun had no good Effect

Effect on my Spiritts: on the Contrarie, nothing in blythe Nature seeming in unison with my Sadnesse, Tears flowed without relieving me.

—— What a solemne, pompous *Prigge* is this Doctor! He cries " humph!" and " aye!" and bites his Nails and screws his Lips together, but I don't believe he understands soe much of Physick, after alle, as Mr. *Agnew.*

Father came Home fulle of the Rebels' Doings, but as for me, I shoulde hear them thundering at our Gate with Apathie, except insofar as I feared them distressing *Robin.*

Audrey rode over with her Father, this Morn, to make Enquiries. She might have come sooner had she meant to be anie reall Use to a Family she has thought of entering. Had *Rose* come to our Help as late in the Day, we had been poorlie off.

Thursday.

Thursday.

MAY *Heaven* in its Mercy save us from the evil Consequence of this new Mischance!—*Richard*, jealous at being allowed so little Share in nursing *Robin*, whom he sayd he loved as well as anie did, would sit up with him last Night, along with *Mother*. Twice I heard him snoring, and stept in to prevail on him to change Places, but coulde not get him to stir. A third Time he fell asleep, and, it seems, *Mother* slept too; and *Robin*, in his Fever, got out of Bed and drank near a Quart of colde Water, waking *Dick* by setting down the Pitcher. Of course the Bustle soon reached my listening Ears. *Dick*, to do him Justice, was frightened enough, and stole away to his Bed without a Word of Defence; but poor *Mother*, who had been equallie off her Watch, made more Noise about it than was good for *Robin*; who, neverthelesse,

thelesse, we having warmlie covered up, burst into a profuse Heat, and fell into a sound Sleep, which hath now holden him manie Hours. Mr. *Agnew* augureth favourablie of his waking, but we await it in prayerfulle Anxietie.

—— The Crisis is past! and the Doctor sayeth he alle along expected it last Night, which I cannot believe, but *Father* and *Mother* doe. At alle Events, praised be *Heaven*, there is now hope that deare *Robin* may recover. *Rose* and I have mingled Tears, Smiles, and Thanksgivings; Mr. *Agnew* hath expressed Gratitude after a more collected Manner, and endeavoured to check the somewhat ill-governed Expression of Joy throughout the House; warning the Servants, but especiallie *Dick* and *Harry*, that *Robin* may yet have a Relapse.

With what Transport have I sat beside dear *Robin's* Bed, returning his fixed, earnest, thankfulle Gaze, and answering the feeble Pressure of his Hand!—Going into the Studdy just now, I found *Father* crying

crying like a Child—the first Time I have known him give Way to Tears during *Robin's* Illnesse. Mr. *Agnew* presentlie came in, and composed him better than I coulde.

Saturday.

OBIN better, though still very weak. Had his Bed made, and took a few Spoonfuls of Broth.

Sunday.

VERY different Sabbath from the last. Though *Robin's* Constitution hath received a Shock it may never recover, his comparative Amendment fills us with Thankfulnesse; and our chastened Suspense hath a sweet Solemnitie and Trustfullenesse in it, which pass Understanding.

Mr. *Agnew* conducted our Devotions. This

This Morning, I found him praying with *Robin*—I question if it were for the first Time. *Robin* looking on him with Eyes of such sedate Affection!

Thursday.

ROBIN still progressing. Dear *Rose* and Mr. *Agnew* leave us tomorrow, but they will soon come agayn. Oh faithful Friends!

. . . .

April, 1646.

CAN Aniething equall the desperate Ingratitude of the human Heart? Testifie of it, Journall, agaynst me. Here did I, throughout the incessant Cares and Anxieties of *Robin's* Sicknesse, find, or make Time, for almoste dailie Record of my Trouble; since which, whole Months have passed without soe much as a scrawled

scrawled Ejaculation of Thankfullenesse that the Sick hath beene made whole.

Yet, not that that Thankfullenesse hath beene unfelt, nor, though unwritten, unexprest. Nay, O *Lord*, deeplie, deeplie have I thanked thee for thy tender Mercies. And he healed soe slowlie, that Suspense, as 'twere wore itself out, and gave Place to a dull, mournful Persuasion that an Hydropsia would waste him away, though more slowlie, yet noe less surelie than the Fever.

Soe Weeks lengthened into Months, I mighte well say Years, they seemed soe long! and stille he seemed to neede more Care and Tendernesse; till, just as he and I had learnt to say, "Thy Will, O *Lord*, "be done," he began to gain Flesh, his craving Appetite moderated, yet his Food nourished him, and by *God's* Blessing he recovered!

During that heavie Season of Probation, our Hearts were unlocked, and we spake oft to one another of Things in Heaven and Things in Earth. Afterwards,

wards, our mutuall Reserves returned, and *Robin*, methinks, became shyer than before, but there can never cease to be a dearer Bond between us. Now we are apart, I aim to keep him mindfulle of the high and holie Resolutions he formed in his Sicknesse; and though he never answers these Portions of my Letters, I am avised to think he finds them not displeasing.

Now that *Oxford* is like to be besieged, my Life is more confined than ever; yet I cannot, and will not leave *Father* and *Mother*, even for the *Agnews*, while they are soe much harassed. This Morning, my Father hath received a Letter from Sir *Thomas Glemham*, requiring a larger Quantitie of winnowed Wheat, than, with alle his Loyaltie, he likes to send.

April.

April 23.

RALPH HEWLETT hath just looked in to say, his Father and Mother have in Safetie reached *London*, where he will shortlie joyn them, and to ask, is there anie Service he can doe me? Ay, truly; one that I dare not name—he can bring me Word of Mr. *Milton*, of his Health, of his Looks, of his Speech, and whether . . .

Ralph shall be noe Messenger of mine.

April 24.

TALKING of Money Matters this Morning, *Mother* sayd Something that brought Tears into mine Eyes. She observed, that though my Husband had never beene a Favourite of hers, there was one Thing wherein she must say he had behaved generously: he had never,

to

to this Day, askt *Father* for the 500*l*. which had brought him, in the first Instance, to *Forest Hill*, (he having promised old Mr. *Milton* to try to get the Debt paid,) and the which, on his asking for my Hand, *Father* tolde him shoulde be made over sooner or later, in lieu of Dower.

Did *Rose* know the Bitter-sweet she was imparting to me, when she gave me, by stealth as 'twere, the latelie publisht Volume of my Husband's *English* Versing? It hath beene my Companion ever since; for I had perused the *Comus* but by Snatches, under the Disadvantage of crabbed Manuscript. This Morning, to use his owne deare Words :—

> *I sat me down to watch, upon a Bank,*
> *With Ivy canopied, and interwove*
> *With flaunting Honeysuckle, and beganne,*
> *Wrapt in a pleasing Fit of Melancholic,*
> *To meditate.*

The Text of my Meditation was this, drawne from the same loved Source :—

This

This I hold firm ;
Virtue may be assayled, but never hurt,
Surprised by unjust Force, but not enthralled ;
Yea, even that which Mischief meant most Harm,
Shall, in the happy Trial, prove most Glory.

But who hath such Virtue? have I? hath he? No, we have both gone astray, and done amiss, and wrought sinfullie; but I worst, I first, therefore more neede that I humble myself, and pray for both.

There is one, more unhappie, perhaps, than either. The *King*, most misfortunate Gentleman! who knoweth not which Way to turn, nor whom to trust. Last Time I saw him, methought never was there a Face soe full of Woe.

May 6.

THE *King* hath escaped! He gave Orders overnight at alle the Gates, for three Persons to passe; and, accompanied onlie by Mr. *Ashburnham,* and Mr. *Hurd,* rode forthe at Nightfalle, towards *London.*

Sure,

Sure, he will not throw himselfe into the Hands of Parliament?

Mother is affrighted beyond Measure at the near Neighbourhood of *Fairfax's* Army, and entreats *Father* to leave alle behind, and flee with us into the City. It may yet be done; and we alle share her Feares.

Saturday Even.

PACKING up in greate haste, after a confused Family Council, wherein some fresh Accounts of the Rebels' Advances, broughte in by *Diggory*, made my Father the sooner consent to a stolen Flight into *Oxford*, *Diggory* being left behind in Charge. Time of Flight, To-morrow after Dark, the *Puritans* being busie at theire Sermons. The better the Day, the better the Deede.—*Heaven* make it soe!

Tuesday.

Tuesday.

OXFORD; in most confined and unpleasant Lodgings; but noe Matter, manie better and richer than ourselves fare worse, and our King hath not where to lay his Head. 'Tis sayd he hath turned his Course towards *Scotland.* There are Souldiers in this House, whose Noise distracts us. Alsoe, a poor Widow Lady, whose Husband hath beene slayn in these Wars. The Children have taken a feverish Complaynt, and require incessant tending. Theire Beds are far from cleane, in too little Space, and ill aired.

May 20.

THE Widow Lady goes about visiting the Sick, and would faine have my Companie. The Streets have displeased me, being soe fulle of Men; however, in a close Hoode I have accompanied

panied her sundrie Times. 'Tis a good Soul, and full of pious Works and Alms-deedes.

May 27.

DIGGORY hath found his Way to us, alle dismaied, and bringing Dismay with him, for the Rebels have taken and ransacked our House, and turned him forthe. " A Plague on these Wars ! " as *Father* says. What are we to doe, or how live, despoyled of alle ? *Father* hath lost, one Way and another, since the Civil War broke out, three thousand Pounds, and is now nearlie beggared. *Mother* weeps bitterlie, and *Father's* Countenance hath fallen more than ever I saw it before. " Nine Children ! " he exclaimed, just now ; " and onlie one " provided for ! " His Eye fell upon me for a Moment, with less Tendernesse than usuall, as though he wished me in

Aldersgate

Aldersgate Street. I'm sure I wish I were there,—not because *Father* is in Misfortune; oh, no.

June.

THE Parliament requireth our unfortunate King to issue Orders to this and alle his other Garrisons, commanding theire Surrender; and *Father*, finding this is likelie to take Place forthwith, is busied in having himself comprised within the Articles of Surrender. 'Twill be hard indeede, shoulde this be denied. His Estate lying in the King's Quarters, how coulde he doe less than adhere to his Majesty's Partie during this unnaturall War? I am sure *Mother* grudged the Royalists everie Goose and Turkey they had from our Yard.

June 27.

PRAISED be *Heaven,* deare *Father* hath just received Sir *Thomas Fairfax's* Protection, empowering him quietlie and without let to goe forthe " with Servants, " Horses, Arms, Goods, etc." to " *London* " or elsewhere," whithersoever he will. And though the Protection extends but over six Months, at the Expiry of which Time, *Father* must take Measures to embark for some Place of Refuge beyond Seas, yet who knows what may turn up in those six Months! The King may enjoy his Owne agayn. Meantime, we immediatelie leave *Oxford.*

Forest Hill.

AT Home agayn; and what a Home! Everiething to seeke, everiething misplaced, broken, abused, or gone altogether! The Gate off its Hinges; the Stone Balls of the Pillars overthrowne, the

the great Bell stolen, the clipt *Junipers* grubbed up, the Sun-diall broken! Not a Hen or Chicken, Duck or Duckling, left. *Crab* half-starved, and soe glad to

see us, that he dragged his Kennel after him. *Daisy* and *Blanch* making such piteous Moans at the Paddock Gate, that I coulde not bear it, but helped *Lettice* to milk

milk them. Within Doors, everie Room smelling of Beer and Tobacco; Cupboards broken open, etc. On my Chamber Floor, a greasy steeple-crowned Hat! Threw it forthe from the Window with a Pair of Tongs.

Mother goes about the House weeping. *Father* sits in his broken Arm-chair, the Picture of Disconsolateness. I see the *Agnews*, true Friends! riding hither; and with them a Third, who, methinks, is *Rose's* Brother *Ralph*.

London.
St. Martin's le Grand.

TREMBLING, weeping, hopefulle, dismaied, here I sit in mine Uncle's hired House, alone in a Crowd, scared at mine owne Precipitation, readie to wish myselfe back, unable to resolve, to reflect, to pray. . . .

Twelve

Twelve at Night.

ALLE is silent; even in the latelie busie Streets. Why art thou cast down, my Heart? why art thou disquieted within me? Hope thou stille in the *Lord*, for he is the Joy and Light of thy Countenance. Thou hast beene long of learning him to be such. Oh, forget not thy Lesson now! Thy best Friend hath sanctioned, nay, counselled this Step, and overcome alle Obstacles, and provided the Means of this Journey; and to-morrow at Noone, if Events prove not cross, I shall have Speech of him whom my Soul loveth. To-night, let me watch, fast, and pray.

Friday

Friday; at Night.

HOW awfulle it is to beholde a Man weepe! mine owne Tears, when I think thereon, well forthe. . . .

Rose was a true Friend when she sayd "our prompt "Affections are oft our wise Counsellors." Soe, she suggested and advised alle; wrung forthe my Father's Consent, and sett me on my Way, even putting Money in my Purse. Well for me, had she beene at my Journey's End as well as its Beginning.

'Stead of which, here was onlie mine Aunt; a slow, timid, uncertayn Soule, who proved but a broken Reed to lean upon.

Soe, alle I woulde have done arighte went crosse, the Letter never delivered, the Message delayed till he had left Home, soe that methought I shoulde goe crazie.

While the Boy, stammering in his lame Excuses,

Excuses, bore my chafed Reproaches the more humblie because he saw he had done me some grievous Hurt, though he knew not what, a Voice in the adjacent Chamber in Alternation with mine Uncle's, drove the Blood of a Suddain from mine Heart, and then sent it back with impetuous Rush, for I knew the Accents right well.

Enters mine Aunt, alle flurried, and hushing her Voice. "Oh, *Niece*, he whom " you wot of is here, but knoweth not " you are at Hand, nor in *London*. Shall " I tell him?"

But I gasped, and held her back by her Skirts; then, with a suddain secret Prayer, or Cry, or maybe, Wish, as 'twere, darted up unto Heaven for Assistance, I took noe Thought what I shoulde speak when confronted with him, but opening the Door between us, he then standing with his Back towards it, rushed forth and to his Feet—there sank, in a Gush of Tears; for not one Word coulde I proffer, nor soe much as look up.

A

"Thus I remained agonized in Tears."

A quick Hand was laid on my Head, on my Shoulder—as quicklie removed . . . and I was aware of the Door being hurriedlie opened and shut, and a Man hasting forthe; but 'twas onlie mine Uncle. Meantime, my Husband, who had at first uttered a suddain Cry or Exclamation, had now left me, sunk on the Ground as I was, and retired a Space, I know not whither, but methinks he walked hastilie to and fro. Thus I remained, agonized in Tears, unable to recal one Word of the humble Appeal I had pondered on my Journey, or to have spoken it, though I had known everie Syllable by Rote; yet not wishing myself, even in that Suspense, Shame, and Anguish, elsewhere than where I was cast, at mine Husband's Feet.

Or ever I was aware, he had come up, and caught me to his Breast: then, holding me back soe as to look me in the Face, sayd, in Accents I shall never forget,

"Much I coulde say to reproach, but
"will not! Henceforth, let us onlie re-
"call

" call this darke Passage of our deeplie
" sinfulle Lives, to quicken us to *God's*
" Mercy in affording us this Re-union.
" Let it deepen our Penitence, enhance
" our Gratitude."

Then, suddainlie covering up his Face with his Hands, he gave two or three Sobs; and for some few Minutes coulde not refrayn himself; but, when at length he uncovered his Eyes and looked down on me with Goodness and Sweetnesse, 'twas like the Sun's cleare shining after Raine. . . .

Shall I now destroy the disgracefulle Records of this blotted Book? I think not; for 'twill quicken me perhaps, as my Husband sayth, to " deeper Penitence " and stronger Gratitude," shoulde I henceforthe be in Danger of settling on the Lees, and forgetting the deepe Waters which had nearlie closed over mine Head. At present, I am soe joyfulle, soe light of Heart under the Sense of Forgivenesse, that it seemeth as though Sorrow coulde
lay

lay hold of me noe more; and yet we are still, as 'twere, disunited for awhile; for my Husband is agayn shifting House, and preparing to move his increased Establishment into *Barbican*, where he hath taken a goodly Mansion; and, until it is ready, I am to abide here. I might pleasantlie cavill at this; but, in Truth, will cavill at Nothing now.

I am, by this, full persuaded that *Ralph's* Tale concerning Miss *Davies* was a false Lie; though, at the Time, supposing it to have some Colour, it inflamed my Jealousie noe little. The cross Spight of that Youth led, under his Sister's Management, to an Issue his Malice never forecast; and now, though I might come at the Truth for Inquiry, I will not soe much as even soil my Mind with thinking of it agayn; for there is that Truth in mine Husband's Eyes, which woulde silence the Slanders of a hundred Liars. Chafed, irritated, he has beene, soe as to excite the sarcastic Constructions of those who wish him evill; but his
Soul,

Soul, and his Heart, and his Mind require a Flighte beyond *Ralph's* Witt to comprehende; and I know and feel that they are *mine*.

He hath just led in the two *Philips's* to me, and left us together. *Jack* lookt at me askance, and held aloof; but deare little *Ned* threw his Arms about me and wept, and I did weep too; seeing the which, *Jack* advanced, gave me his Hand, and finally his Lips, then lookt as much as to say, " Now, Alle's right." They are grown, and are more comely than heretofore, which, in some Measure, is owing to theire Hair being noe longer cut strait and short after the Puritanicall Fashion I soe hate, but curled like their Uncle's.

I have writ, not the Particulars, but the Issue of my Journey, unto *Rose*, whose loving Heart, I know, yearns for Tidings. Alsoe, more brieflie unto my Mother, who loveth not Mr. *Milton*.

Barbican,

Barbican, September.

IN the Night-season, we take noe Rest; we search out our Hearts, and commune with our Spiritts, and checque our Souls' Accounts, before we dare court our Sleep; but in the Day of Happinesse we cut shorte our Reckonings; and here am I, a joyfulle Wife, too proud and busie amid my dailie Cares to have leisure for more than a brief Note in my *Diarium*, as *Ned* woulde call it. 'Tis a large House, with more Rooms than we can fill, even with the *Philips's* and their Scholar-mates, olde Mr. *Milton*, and my Husband's Books to boot. I feel Pleasure in being housewifelie; and reape the Benefit of alle that I learnt of this Sorte at *Sheepscote*. Mine Husband's Eyes follow me with Delight; and once with a perplexed yet pleased Smile, he sayd to me, "Sweet Wife, thou art "strangelie altered; it seems as though
"I

"I have indeede lost 'sweet *Moll*' after "Alle!"

Yes, I am indeed changed; more than he knows or coulde believe. And he is changed too. With Payn I perceive a more stern, severe Tone occasionallie used by him; doubtlesse the Cloke assumed by his Griefe to hide the Ruin I had made within. Yet a more geniall Influence is fast melting this away. Agayn, I note with Payn that he complayns much of his Eyes. At first, I observed he rubbed them oft, and dared not mention it, believing that his Tears on Account of me, sinfulle Soule! had made them smart. Soe, perhaps, they did in the first Instance, for it appears they have beene ailing ever since the Year I left him; and Overstuddy, which my Presence mighte have prevented, hath conduced to the same ill Effect. Whenever he now looks at a lighted Candle, he sees a Sort of Iris alle about it; and, this Morning, he disturbed me by mentioning that a total Darknesse obscured everie Thing on the left Side of of his Eye, and that he even feared, sometimes, he might eventuallie lose the Sight of both. " In which Case," he cheerfully sayd, " you, deare Wife, must become my " Lecturer as well as Amanuensis, and " content yourself to read to me a World " of crabbed Books, in Tongues that are " not nor neede ever be yours, seeing that " a Woman has ever Enough of her own !"

Then, more pensivelie, he added, " I " discipline and tranquillize my Mind on " this Subject, ever remembering, when " the Apprehension afflicts me, that, as " Man lives not by Bread alone, but by " everie Word that proceeds out of the " Mouth of *God*, so Man likewise lives " not by *Sight* alone, but by Faith in the " Giver of Sight. As long, therefore, as " it shall please Him to prolong, however " imperfectlie, this precious Gift, soe long " will I lay up Store agaynst the Days " of Darknesse, which may be many ; and " whensoever it shall please Him to with-" drawe it from me altogether, I will " cheerfully bid mine Eyes keep Holiday,
" and

" and place my Hand trustfullie in His,
" to be led whithersoever He will, through
" the Remainder of Life."

A Honeymoon cannot for ever last;
nor Sense of Danger, when it long hath
past;—but one little Difference from out
manie greater Differences between my late
happie Fortnighte in *St. Martin's-le-Grand*,
and my present dailie Course in *Barbican*,
hath marked the Distinction between
Lover and Husband. There it was "sweet
" *Moll*," " my Heart's Life of Life," " my
" dearest cleaving Mischief;" here 'tis
onlie " Wife," " Mistress *Milton*," or at
most " deare or sweet Wife." This, I
know, is masterfulle and seemly.

Onlie, this Morning, chancing to quote
one of his owne Lines,

These Things may startle well, but not astounde,—

he sayd, in a Kind of Wonder, " Why,
" *Moll*, whence had you that?— Me-
" thought you hated Versing, as you used
" to call it. When learnt you to love
" it?"

"it?" I hung my Head in my old foolish Way, and answered, "Since I "learnt to love the Verser." "Why, "this is the best of Alle!" he hastilie cried, "Can my sweet Wife be indeede "Heart of my Heart and Spirit of my "Spirit? I lost, or drove away a Child, "and have found a Woman." Thereafter, he less often wifed me, and I found I was agayn sweet *Moll*.

This Afternoon, *Christopher Milton* lookt in on us. After saluting me with the usuall Mixture of Malice and Civilitie in his Looks, he fell into easie Conversation; and presentlie says to his Brother quietlie enough, "I saw a curious Penny-worth at "a Book-stall as I came along this Morn-"ing." "What was that?" says my Husband, brightening up. "It had a "long Name," says *Christopher*,—"I think "it was called *Tetrachordon*." My Husband cast at me a suddain, quick Look, but I did not soe much as change Colour; and quietlie continued my Sewing.

"I wonder," says he, after a Pause, "that

"that you did not invest a small Portion of your Capitall in the Work, as you say 'twas soe greate a Bargain. However, Mr. *Kit*, let me give you one small Hint with alle the goode Humour imaginable; don't take Advantage of our neare and deare Relation to make too frequent Opportunities of saying to me Anything that would certainlie procure for another Man a Thrashing!"

Then, after a short Silence betweene Alle, he suddainlie burst out laughing, and cried, "I know 'tis on the Stalls; I've seene it, *Kit*, myself! Oh, had you seene, as I did, the Blockheads poring over the Title, and hammering at it while you might have walked to *Mile End* and back!"

"That's Fame, I suppose," says *Christopher* drylie; and then goes off to talk of some new Exercise of the Press-licenser's Authoritie, which he seemed to approve, but it kindled my Husband in a Minute.

"What Folly! what Nonsense!" cried he, smiting the Table; "these *Jacks* in Office

"Office sometimes devise such senselesse
"Things that I really am ashamed of
"being of theire Party. Licence, in-
"deed! their Licence! I suppose they
"will shortlie license the Lengthe of
"*Moll's* Curls, and regulate the Colour
"of her Hoode, and forbid the Larks to
"sing within Sounde of *Bow Bell*, and
"the Bees to hum o' *Sundays*. Me-
"thoughte I had broken *Mabbot's* Teeth
"two Years agone; but I must bring
"forthe a new Edition of my *Areopa-
"gitica;* and I'll put your Name down,
"*Kit*, for a hundred Copies!"

October.

THOUGH a rusticall Life hath ever had my Suffrages, Nothing can be more pleasant than our regular Course. We rise at five or sooner: while my Husband combs his Hair, he commonly hums or sings some Psalm or Hymn, versing it, maybe, as he goes on.
Being

Being drest, *Ned* reads him a Chapter in the *Hebrew* Bible. With *Ned* stille at his Knee, and me by his Side, he expounds and improves the Same; then, after a shorte, heartie Prayer, releases us both. Before I have finished my Dressing, I hear him below at his Organ, with the two lads, who sing as well as Choristers, hymning Anthems and *Gregorian* Chants, now soaring up to the Clouds, as 'twere, and then dying off as though some wide echoing Space lay betweene us. I usuallie find Time to tie on my Hoode and slip away to the Herb-market for a Bunch of fresh Radishes or Cresses, a Sprig of Parsley, or at the leaste a Posy, to lay on his Plate. A good wheaten Loaf, fresh Butter and Eggs, and a large Jug of Milk, compose our simple Breakfast; for he likes not, as my Father, to see Boys hacking a huge Piece of Beef, nor cares for heavie feeding, himself. Onlie, olde Mr. *Milton* sometimes takes a Rasher of toasted Bacon, but commonly, a Basin of Furmity, which I prepare

more

more to his Minde than the Servants can.

After Breakfast, I well know the Boys' Lessons will last till Noone. I therefore goe to my Closett Duties after my *Forest Hill* Fashion; thence to Market, buy what I neede, come Home, look to my Maids, give forthe needfulle Stores, then to my Needle, my Books, or perchance to my Lute, which I woulde faine play better. From twelve to one is the Boys' Hour of Pastime; and it may generallie be sayd, my Husband's and mine too. He draws aside the green Curtain,—for we sit mostly in a large Chamber shaped like the Letter T, and thus divided while at our separate Duties: my End is the pleasantest, has the Sun most upon it, and hath a Balcony overlooking a Garden. At one, we dine; always on simple, plain Dishes, but drest with Neatnesse and Care. Olde Mr. *Milton* sits at my right Hand and says Grace; and, though growing a little deaf, enters into alle the livelie Discourse at Table. He loves me to help him

him to the tenderest, by Reason of his Losse of Teeth. My Husband careth not to sitt over the Wine; and hath noe sooner finished the Cheese and Pippins than he reverts to the Viol or Organ, and not onlie sings himself, but will make me sing too, though he sayth my Voice is better than my Ear. Never was there such a tunefulle Spiritt. He alwaies tears himself away at laste, as with a Kind of Violence, and returns to his Books at six o' the Clock. Meantime, his old Father dozes, and I sew at his Side.

From six to eight, we are seldom without Friends, chance Visitants, often scholarlike and witty, who tell us alle the News, and remain to partake a light Supper. The Boys enjoy this Season as much as I doe, though with Books before them, their Hands over their Ears, pretending to con the Morrow's Tasks. If the Guests chance to be musicalle, the Lute and Viol are broughte forthe, to alternate with Roundelay and Madrigal: the old Man beating Time with his feeble Fingers,

Fingers, and now and then joining with his quavering Voice. (By the way, he hath not forgotten to this Hour, my imputed Crime of losing that Song by *Harry Lawes:* my Husband takes my Part, and sayth it will turn up some Day when leaste expected, like *Justinian's Pandects.*) *Hubert* brings him his Pipe and a Glass of Water; and then I crave his Blessing and goe to Bed; first, praying ferventlie for alle beneathe this deare Roof, and then for alle at *Sheepscote* and *Forest Hill.*

On Sabbaths, besides the publick Ordinances of Devotion, which I cannot, with alle my striving, bring myself to love like the Services to which I have beene accustomed, we have much Reading, Singing, and Discoursing among ourselves. The Maids sing, the Boys sing, *Hubert* sings, olde Mr. *Milton* sings; and trulie with soe much of it, I woulde sometimes as lief have them quiete. The *Sheepscote* Sundays suited me better. The Sabbath Exercise of the Boys is to read a Chapter in the *Greek* Testament, heare my Husband

band expounde the same; and write out a System of Divinitie as he dictates to them, walking to and fro. In listening thereto, I find my Pleasure and Profitt.

I have alsoe my owne little Catechising, after a humbler Sorte, in the Kitchen, and some poore Folk to relieve and console, with my Husband's Concurrence and Encouragement.

Encouragement. Thus, the Sabbath is devoutlie and happilie passed.

My Husband alsoe takes, once in a Fortnighte or soe, what he blythelie calls "a gaudy Day," equallie to his owne Content, the Boys', and mine. On these Occasions, it is my Province to provide colde Fowls or Pigeon Pie, which *Hubert* carries, with what else we neede, to the Spot selected for our Camp Dinner. Sometimes we take Boat to *Richmond* or *Greenwich*. Two young Gallants, Mr. *Alphrey* and Mr. *Miller*, love to joyn our Partie, and toil at the Oar, or scramble up the Hills, as merrilie as the Boys. I must say they deal savagelie with the Pigeon Pie afterwards. They have as wild Spiritts as our *Dick* and *Harry*, but withal a most wonderfull Reverence for my Husband, whom they courte to read and recite, and provoke to pleasant Argument, never prolonged to Wearinesse, and seasoned with frolic Jest and Witt. Olde Mr. *Milton* joyns not these Parties. I leave him alwaies to *Dolly's* Care, firste providing

providing for him a Sweetbread or some smalle Relish, such as he loves. He is in Bed ere we Return, which is oft by Moonlighte.

How soone must Smiles give Way to Tears! Here is a Letter from deare *Mother*, taking noe Note of what I write to her, and for good Reason, she is soe distraught at her owne and deare *Father's* ill Condition. The Rebels (I must call them such,) have soe stript and opprest them, they cannot make theire House tenantable; nor have Aught to feede on, had they e'en a whole Roof over theire Heads. The Neighbourhoode is too hot to holde them; olde Friends cowardlie and suspicious, olde and new Foes in League together. Leave *Oxon* they must; but where to goe? *Father*, despite his broken Health and Hatred of the Foreigner, must needes depart beyond Seas; at leaste within the six Months; but how, with an emptie Purse, make his Way in a strange Land, with a Wife and seven Children at his Heels?

Heels? Soe ends *Mother* with a " *Lord*
" have Mercy upon us!" as though her
House were as surelie doomed to Destruction as if it helde the Plague.

Mine Eyes were yet swollen with
Tears, when my Husband stept in. He
askt, "What ails you, precious Wife?"
I coulde but sigh, and give him the
Letter. Having read the Same, he says,
" But what, my dearest? Have we not
" ample Room here for them alle? I
" speak as to Generalls, you must care for
" Particulars, and stow them as you will.
" There are plenty of small Rooms for
" the Boys; but, if your Father, being
" infirm, needes a Ground-floor Chamber,
" you and I will mount aloft."

I coulde but look my Thankfullenesse
and kiss his Hand. "Nay," he added,
with increasing Gentlenesse, "think not
" I have seene your Cares for my owne
" Father without loving and blessing you.
" Let Mr. *Powell* come and see us happie;
" it may tend to make him soe. Let him
" and his abide with us, at the leaste, till
" the

"the Spring; his Lads will studdy and
"play with mine, your Mother will help
"you in your Housewiferie, the two
"olde Men will chrip together beside the
"*Christmasse* Hearth; and, if I find thy
"Weeklie Bills the heavier 'twill be but
"to write another Book, and make a
"better Bargain for it than I did for the
"last. We will use Hospitalitie without
"grudging; and, as for your owne In-
"crease of Cares, I suppose 'twill be but
"to order two Legs of Mutton insteade
"of one!"

And soe, with a Laugh, left me, most joyfulle, happy Wife! to drawe Sweete out of Sowre, Delighte out of Sorrowe; and to summon mine owne Kindred aboute me, and wipe away theire Tears, bid them eat, drink, and be merry, and shew myselfe to them, how proud, how cherished a Wife!

Surelie my Mother will learne to love *John Milton* at last! If she doth not, this will be my secret Crosse, for 'tis hard to love dearlie two Persons who esteeme

esteeme not one another. But she will, she must, not onlie respect him for his Uprightnesse and Magnanimitie, coupled with what himselfe calls "an honest "Haughtinesse and Self-esteeme," but *like* him for his kind and equall Temper, (*not* "harsh and crabbed," as I have hearde her call it,) his easie Flow of Mirthe, his Manners, unaffectedlie cheerfulle; his Voice, musicall; his Person, beautifull; his Habitt, gracefull; his Hospitalitie, naturall to him; his Purse, Countenance, Time, Trouble, at his Friend's Service; his Devotion, humble; his Forgivenesse, heavenlie! May it please *God* that my Mother shall like *John Milton!* . . . .

Deborah's Diary
A Sequel to "Mary Powell"

DEBORAH'S DIARY

A FRAGMENT

Bunhill Fields, Feb. 17, 1665.

. . . . . .

SOMETHING geniall and soothing beyond ordinarie in the Warmth and fitfulle Lighte of the Fire, made us delaye, I know not how long, to trim the Evening Lamp, and sitt muzing in Idlenesse about the Hearth ; *Mary* revolving her Thumbs and staring at the Embers ; *Anne* quite in the Shadowe, with her Arms behind her Head agaynst the Wall ; Father in his tall Arm-chair, quite uprighte, as his Fashion is when very thoughtfulle ; I on the Cushion at his Feet,

Feet, with mine Head on's Knee and mine Eyes on his Shadowe on the Wall, which, as it happened, shewed in colossal Proportions, while ours were like Pigmies. Alle at once he exclaims, "We all seem "very comfortable—I think we shoulde "reward ourselves with some Egg-flip!"

And then offered us Pence for our Thoughts. *Anne* would not tell hers; *Mary* owned she had beene trying to account for the Deficiencie of a Groat in her housekeeping Purse; and I confest to such a Medley, that Father sayd I deserved *Anne's* Penny in addition to mine own, for my Strength of Mind in submitting such a Farrago of Nonsense to the Ridicule of my Friends.

Soe then I bade for his Thoughts, and he sayd he had beene questioning the Cricket on the Hearth, upon the Extinction of the Fairies; and I askt, Did anie believe in 'em now? and he made Answer, Oh, yes, he had known a Serving-Wench in Oxon depone she had beene nipped and haled by 'em; and, of Crickets, he sayd

sayd he had manie Times seene an old Wife in *Buckinghamshire*, who was soe pestered by one, that she cried, " I can't " heare myself talk ! I'd as lief heare " Nought as heare thee ; " soe poured a Kettle of boiling Water into the Cranny wherein the harmlesse Creature lay, and scalded it to death ; and, the next Day, became as deaf as a Stone, and remained soe ever after, a Monument of God's Displeasure, at her destroying one of the most innocent of His Creatures.

After this, he woulde tell us of this and that worn-out Superstition, as o' the Friar's Lantern, and of Lob-lie-by-the-Fire, untill *Mary*, who affects not the Unreall, went off to make the Flip. *Anne* presentlie exclaimed, " Father ! " when you sayd—

> ' The Shepherds on the Lawn,
> ' Or e'er the Point of Dawn,
>   ' Sat simply chatting in a rustic Row,
> ' Full little thought they then
> ' That the mighty Pan
>   ' Was kindly come to live with them below,'

" whom

"whom meant you by *Pan*? Sure, you
"would not call our Lord by the Name
"of a heathen Deity?"

"Well, Child," returns Father, "you
"know He calls Himself a Shepherd,
"and was in truth what *Pan* was onlie
"supposed to be, the God of Shepherds;
"albeit *Lavaterus*, in his Treatise *De Le-*
"*muribus*, doth indeede tell us, that by
"*Pan* some understoode noe other than
"the great *Sathanas*, whose Kingdom
"being overturned at *Christ's* Coming,
"his inferior Demons expelled, and his
"Oracles silenced, he in some sort was
"himself overthrown. And the Story
"goes, that, about the Time of our
"Lord's Passion, certain Persons sailing
"from *Italy* to *Cyprus*, and passing by
"certayn Islands, did heare a Voice call-
"ing aloud, *Thamus, Thamus*, which was
"the Name of the Ship's Pilot, who,
"making Answer to the unseene Appel-
"lant, was bidden, when he came to
"*Palodas*, to tell that the great God
"*Pan* was dead; which he doubting to
"doe,

"doe, yet for that when he came to
"*Palodas*, there suddainlie was such a
"Calm of Wind that the Ship stoode
"still in the Sea, he was constrayned
"to cry aloud that *Pan* was dead;
"whereupon there were hearde such
"piteous Shrieks and Cries of Invisible
"Beings, echoing from haunted Spring
"and Dale, as ne'er smote human Ears
"before nor since: Nymphs and Wood-
"Gods, or they that had passed for such,
"breaking up House and retreating to
"their own Place. I warrant you, there
"was Trouble among the Sylvan People
"that Day—Satyrs hirsute and cloven-
"footed Fauns.

". . . Many a Time and oft have
"*Charles Diodati* and I discust fond
"Legends, such as this, over our Winter
"Hearth; with our Chestnuts blacken-
"ing and crackling on the Hob, and our
"o'er-ripe Pears sputtering in the Fire,
"while the Wind raved without among
"the creaking Elms. . . ."

Father still hammering on old Times,
and

and his owne young Days, I beganne to frame unto myself an Image of what he might then have beene; piecing it out by Help of his Picture on the Wall; but coulde get no cleare Apprehension of my Mother, she dying soe untimelie. Askt him, Was she beautifulle? He sayth, Oh yes, and clouded over o' the suddain; then went over her Height, Size, and Colour, etc.; dwelt on the Generalls of personal Beauty, how it shadowed forthe the Mind, was desirable or dangerous, etc.

On dispersing for the Night, he noted, somewhat hurt, *Anne's* abrupt Departure without kissing his Hand, and sayd, "Is " she sulky or unwell?"

In our Chamber, found her alreadie half undrest, a reading of her Bible; sayd, " Father tooke your briefe Good-nighte " amisse." She made Answer shortlie, " Well, what neede to marvell; he can- " not put his Arm about me without " being reminded how mis-shapen I am."

Poor *Nan!* we had been speaking of faire Proportions, and had thoughtlessly cut

cut her to the Quick; yet Father *knoweth*, though he cannot *see*, that her Face is that of an Angel.

BOUT One o' the Clock, was rouzed (though *Anne* continued sleeping soundly) by hearing Father give his three Signal-taps agaynst the Wall. Half drest, and with bare Feet thrust into Slippers, I hastily ran in to him; he cried, "*Deb*, for "the Love of Heaven get Pen and Paper "to sett Something down." I replied, "Sure, Father, you gave me quite a Turn; "I thought you were ill," and sett to my Task, marvellous ill-conditioned, expecting some Crotchet had taken him concerning his Will.

'Stead of which, out comes a Volley of Poetry he had lain a brewing till his Brain was like to burst; and soe I, in my thin Night Cotes, must needs jot it all down, for Feare it should ooze away
before

before Morning. Sure, I thought he

never would get to the End, and really
feared

feared at firste he was crazing a little, but indeede all Poets doe when the Vein is on 'em. At length, with a Sigh of Relief, he says, "That will doe—Good-"night, little Maid." I coulde not help saying, "'Twas a lucky Thing for you, "Father, that Step-mother was from "Home;" he laught, drew me to him, kissed me, and sayd, "Why, your Face is "quite cold; are your Feet unslippered?"

"Unstockinged," I replyed.

"I am quite concerned I knew it not "sooner," he rejoyned, in an Accent of such Kindnesse, that all my Vexation melted away, and I e'en protested I did not mind it a Bit.

"Since it is soe," quoth he, "I shall "the less mind having Recourse to you "agayn; onlie I must insist on your "taking Care to wrap yourself up more "warmly, since you need not feare my "being ill."

I bit my Lip, and onlie saying Goodnight, stole off to my warm Bed.

RETURNING

ETURNING from Morning Prayers with *Anne* this Forenoon, I found *Mary* mending a Pen with the utmoste Imperturbabilitie, and Father with a Heat-spot on his Cheek, which betraied some Inquietation. Being presentlie alone with him, "*Mary* is irretrievably heavy," sighs he, "she would let the finest Thought "escape one while she is blowing her "Nose or brushing up the Cinders. I "am confident she has beene writing "Nonsense even now—Do run through "it for me, *Deb*, and lett me heare what "it is."

I went on, enough to his Satisfaction, till coming to

"*Bring to their Sweetness no Sobriety.*"

"Sobriety?" interrupted he, "Satiety, "Satiety! the Blockhead!—and that I "should live to call a Woman soe.— "Sobriety, indeede! poor *Mary*, her "Wits

"Wits must have been wool-gathering.
"'Bring to their Sweetness no Sobriety!'
"What Meaning coulde she possibly affix
"to such Folly?"

"Sure, Father," sayd I, "here's Enough
"that she could affix no Meaning to, nor
"I neither, without your condescending
"to explayn it—Cycle, Epicycle, noc-
"turnal Rhomb."

"Well, well," returned he, beginning
to smile, "'twas unlikely she shoulde be
"with such Discourse delighted. Not
"capable, alas! poor *Mary's* Ear, of what
"is high. And yet, thy Mother, Child,
"woulde have stretched up towards
"Truths, though beyond her Reach, yet
"to the inquiring Mind offering rich
"Repast. And now write Satiety for
"Sobriety, if you love me."

While erasing the obnoxious Word, I
cried, "Dear Father, pray answer me one
"Question—What is a Rhomb?"

"A Rhomb, Child?" repeated he,
laughing, "why, a Parallelogram or quad-
"rangular Figure, consisting of parallel
"Lines,

" Lines, with two acute and two obtuse
" Angles, and formed by two equal and
" righte Cones, joyned together at their
" Base ! There, are you anie wiser now ?
" No, little Maid, 'tis best for such as
" you
    Not with perplexing Thoughts
To interrupt the Sweet of Life, from which
God hath bid dwell far off all anxious Cares,
And not molest us, unless we ourselves
Seek them, with wandering Thoughts and
  Notions vain."

April 19.

I HEARTILIE wish our Stepmother were back, albeit we are soe comfortable without her ! *Mary,* taking the Maids at unawares last Night, found a strange Man in the Kitchen. Words ensued; he slunk off like a Culprit, which lookt not well, while *Betty Fisher,* brazening it out, woulde have at firste that he was her Brother, then her Cousin, and ended by vowing to be revenged on
            Mary

Mary when she lookt not for it. I would have had *Mary* speak to Father, but she will not; perhaps soe best. *Polly* is in the Sulks to Daye, as well as *Betty*, saying, " As well live in a Nunnerie."

April 20.

WHEN the Horse is stolen, shut the Stable Door. *Mary* locked the lower Doors, and brought up the Keys herselfe, yestereven at Duske. Anon dropped in Doctor *Paget*, Mr. *Skinner*, and Uncle *Dick*, soe that we had quite a merrie Party. Dr. *Paget* sayd how that another Case of the Plague had occurred in *Long Acre;* howbeit, this onlie makes three, soe that we trust it will not spread, though 'twoulde be unadvised to goe needlesslie into the infected Quarter. Uncle *Dick* would fayn take us Girls down to *Oxon*, but Father sayd he could not spare us while Mother was at *Stoke;* and that there was noe prevalent Distemper, this bracing Weather, in in our Parish. Then felle a musing; and Uncle *Dick*, who loves a Jeste, outs with a large brown Apple from's Pocket, and holds it aneath Father's Nose. Sayth Father, rousing, "How far Phansy goes! "thy Voice, *Dick*, carried me back to "olde Dayes, and affected, I think, even "my Nose; for I could protest I smelled "a *Sheepscote* Apple." And, feeling him-selfe touched by its cold Skin, laught merrilie, and ate it with a Relish; saying, noe Sorte ever seemed unto him soe goode—he had received manie a Hamper of 'em about Christmasse. After a Time, alle but he and I went up, and out on the Leads, to see the Comet; and we two sitting quite still, and Father, doubtlesse, supposed to be alone, I saw a great round-shouldered mannish Shadowe glide across the Passage, and hearde the Front-door Latch click. Darted forthe, but too late, and then into the Kitchen; with some Warmth chid *Betty* for soe soone agayn disobeying Orders, and threatened to tell my Mamma. She cryed pertlie, "Law,

"Law, Miss *Deb*, I wish to Goodnesse your Mamma was here to heare you, for I'd sooner have one Mistress than three. A Shadowe, indeede! I'm sure you saw no Substance—very like, 'twas a Spirit; or, liker still, onlie the Cat. Here, Puss, Puss!"... and soe into the Passage, as though to look for what she was sure not to find. I had noe Patience with her; but, returning to Father, askt him if he had not heard the Latch click? He sayd, No; and, indeede, I think, had been dozing; soe then sate still, and bethoughte me what 'twere best to doe. Three Brains are too little agaynst one that is resolved to cheat. 'Tis noe Goode complayning to a Man; he will not see, even though unafflicted like Father, who cannot. Men's Minds run on greater Things, and soe they are fretted at domestic Appeals, and generallie give Judgment the wrong Way. Thus we founde it before, poor motherlesse Girls, to our Cost; and I reallie believe it was more in Kindnesse for us than

than himself, that Father listened to the Doctor's Overtures in behalfe of Miss *Minshull;* for what Companion can soe illiterate a Woman be to him? But he believed her gentle, hearde that she was a good Housewife, and apprehended she would be kind to us. . . . Alas the Daye! What Tears we three shed in our Chamber that Night! and wished, too late, we had ne'er referred to him a Grievance, nor let him know we had a Burthen. Soone we founde King *Log* had been succeeded by King *Stork;* soone made common Cause, tryed our Strength and found it wanting, and soone submitted to our new Yoke, and tried to make the best of it.

Yes, that is the onlie Course; we alle feele it; onlie, as Ill-luck will have it, we do not always feel it simultaneouslie. *Anne,* mayhap, has one of her dogged humours; *Mary* and I see how much better 'twould be, did she overcome it, or shut herself up till in better Temper. *Mary* is crabbed and exacting; *Anne* and

I

I cannot put her straight. Well for us when we succeed just soe far as to keep it from the Notice of Father. Thus we rub on; I wonder if we ever shall pull all together?

April 22.

LIKE unto a wise Masterbuilder, who ordereth the Disposition of eache Stone till the whole Building is fitly compacted together, so doth Father build up his noble Poem, which groweth under our Hands. Three Nights have I, without Complaynt, lost my Rest while writing at his Bedside; this hath made me yawnish in the Day-time, or, as Mother will have it, lazy. However, I bethink me of *Damo*, Daughter of *Pythagoras*.

Mother came Home yesterday, and *Betty*, the Picture of Neatnesse, tooke goode Heede to be the first to welcome her, with officious Smiles, and Prayses of her Looks. For my Part, I thoughte it fullsome,

fullsome, but knew her Motives better than Mother, who took it alle in goode Part. Indeede, noe one would give this Girl credit for soe false a Heart; she is pretty, modest looking, and for a while before my Father's Marriage was as great a Favourite with *Mary* as now with my Mother; flattered her the same, and tempted her to idle gossiping Confidences. She was slow to believe herself cheated; and when 'twas as cleare as Day, could not convince Father of it.

On *Mary's* mentioning this Morning (unadvisedlie, I think,) the Kitchen Visitor, Mother made short Answer—

"Tilly-vally! bad Mistresses make bad "Maids; there will be noe such Doings "now, I warrant. . . . I am sure, my "Dear," appealing to Father, "you think "well in the main of *Betty*?"

"Yes," says he, smiling, "I think well "of both my *Betties*."

"At any rate," persists *Mary*, "the "Man coulde not be at once her Cousin "and her Brother."

"Why

"Why no," replies Father, "therein she worsened her Story, by saying too much, as *Dorothea* did, when she pretended to have heard of the Knight of *La Mancha's* Fame, when she landed at *Ossuna*; which even a Madman as he was, knew to be noe Sea-port. It requires more Skill than the General possess, to lie with a Circumstance."

AD a Valentine this Morning, though onlie from *Ned Phillips*, whom Mother is angry with, for filling my Head betimes with such Nonsense. Howbeit, I am close on sixteen.

Mary was out of Patience with Father yesterday, who, after keeping her a full Hour at *Thucydides*, sayd,

"Well, now we will refresh ourselves with a Canto of *Ariosto*," which was as much a sealed Book to her as t'other. Howbeit, this Morning he sayd,

"Child,

"Child, I have noted your Wearinesse in reading the dead Languages to me; would that I needed not to be beholden unto any, whether bound to me by Blood and Affection or not, for the Food that is as needfulle to me as my daily Bread. Nevertheless, that I be not further wearisome unto thee, I have engaged a young *Quaker*, named *Ell-wood*, to relieve thee of this Portion of thy Task, soe that thou mayst have the more Leisure to enjoy the glad Sunshine and fair Sights I never more shall see."

Mary turned red, and dropt a quiet Tear; but alas, he knew it not.

"One part of my Children's Burthen, indeed," he continued, "I cannot, for obvious Reasons, relieve them of—they must still be my Secretaries, for in them alone can I confide. Soe now to your healthfulle Exercises and fitting Recreations, dear Maids, and Heaven's Blessing goe with you!"

We kissed his Hand and went, but our Walk was not merry.

Ellwood

Ellwood is a young Man of seven-and-twenty, of good Parts, but pragmaticalle; Son of an Oxfordshire Justice of the Peace, but not on good Terms with him, by Reason of his religious Opinions, which the Father affects not.

April 23.

SPRING is coming on apace. Father even sits between the wood Fire and the open Casement, enjoying the mild Air, but it is not considered healthfulle.

" My Dear," says Mother to him this Morning, after some Hours' Absence, " I " have bought me a new Mantle of the " most absolute Fancy. 'Tis sad-coloured, " which I knew you would approve, but " with a Garniture of Orange-tawny; " three Plaits at the Waist behind, and a " little stuck-up Collar."

" You are a comical Woman," says Father, " to spend soe much Money and " Mind

"Mind on a Thing your Husband will never see."

"Oh! but it cost no Money at alle," says she; "that is the best of it."

"What is the best of it?" rejoyned he. "I suppose you bartered for it, if you did not buy it—you Women are always for cheap Pennyworths. Come, what was the Ransom? One of my old Books, or my new Coat?"

"Your last new Coat may be called old too, I'm sure," says Mother; "I believe you married me in it."

"Nay," says Father, "and what if I did? 'Twas new then, at any rate; and the Cid *Ruy Diaz* was married in a black Satin Doublet, which his Father had worn in three or four Battles."

"A poor Compliment to the Bride," says Mother.

"Well, but, dear *Betty*, what has gone for this copper-coloured Mantle?— *Sylvester's* 'Du Bartas'?" . . .

"Nothing of the sort,—nothing you value or will ever miss. An old Gold Pocket-piece,

"Pocket-piece, that hath lain perdue, e'er
"soe long, in our Dressing-table Drawer."

He smote the Table with his Hand.
"Woman!" cried he, changing Colour,
"'twas a Medal of Honour given to my
"Father by a Polish Prince! It should
"have been an Heir-loom. There, say
"noe more about it now. 'Tis in your
"Jew's Furnace ere this. 'The Fining-
"pot for Silver and the Furnace for Gold,
"but . . . the Lord trieth the Spirits.'
"Ay me! mine is tried sometimes."

Uncle *Kit* most opportunelie entering at this Moment, instantaneouslie changed his Key-note.

"Ha, *Kit!*" he cries, gladly, "here you
"find me, as usual, maundering among
"my Women. Welcome, welcome!
"How is it with you, and what's the
"News?"

"Why, the News is, that the Plague's
"coming on amain," says my Uncle;
"they say it's been smouldering among
"us all the Winter, and now it's bursting
"out."

"Lord

"Lord save us!" says Mother, turning pale.

"You may say that," says Uncle, "but "you must alsoe try to save yourselves. "For my Part, I see not what shoulde "keep you in Town. Come down to us "at *Ipswich;* my Brother and you shall "have the haunted Chamber; and we "can make plenty of Shakedowns for the "Girls in the Atticks. Your Maids can "look after Matters here. By the way, "you have a Merlin's Head sett up in "your Neighbourhood; I saw your black- "eyed Maid come forthe of it as I "passed."

Mother bit her Lip; but Father broke forthe with, "What can we expect but "that a judiciall Punishment shoulde be- "fall a Land where the Corruption of "the Court, more potent and subtile in "its Infection than anie Pestilence, hath "tainted every open Resorte and bye "Corner of the Capital and Country? "Our Sins cry aloud; our Pulpits, Coun- "ters, and Closetts alike witness against "us.

"us. 'Tis, as with the People soe with
"the Priest, as with the Buyer soe with the
"Seller, as with the Maid soe with the
"Mistress. Plays, Interludes, Gaming-
"houses, Sabbath Debauches, Dancing-
"rooms, Merry-Andrews, Jack Puddings,
"Quacks, false Prophesyings—"

"Ah! we can excuse a little Bitter-
"nesse in the losing Party now," says
Uncle; "but do you seriously mean to
"say you think us more deserving of
"judiciall Punishment under the glorious
"Restoration than during the unnatural
"Rebellion? Sure you have had Time
"to cool upon that."

"Certainly I mean to say so," answers
Father. "During the unnatural Rebel-
"lion, as you please to call it, the Com-
"monwealth, whose Duration was very
"short—"

"Very short, indeed," observes Uncle,
coughing. "Only from *Worcester* Fight,
"Fifty-one, to *Noll's* Dissolution of the
"Long Parliament, Fifty-three; yet quite
"long enough to see what it was."

"I

"I deny that, as well as your Dates," says Father. "We enjoyed a Common-wealth under the Protector, who, had he not assumed that high Office which gave him his Name, would have lacked Opportunity of showing that he was capable of filling the most exalted Station with Vigour and Ability. He secured a Wise Peace, obtained the respectfull Concurrence of foreign Powers, filled our domestick Courts with upright Judges, and respected the Rights of Conscience."

"Why, suppose I admitted all this, which I am far from doing," says Uncle, "what was he but a King, except by just Title? What had become, meantime, of your Commonwealth?"

"Softly, *Kit*," returns Father. "The Commonwealth was progressing, meantime, like a little Rivulet that rises among the Hills, amid Weeds and Moss, and gradually works itself a widening Channel, filtering over Beds of Gravel, and obstructed here and there by

"by Fragments of Rock, that sorely chafe
"and trouble it, at the very Time that,
"to the distant Observer, it looks most
"picturesque and beautiful."

"Well, I suppose I was never distant
"enough to see it in this picturesque
"Point of View," says Uncle. "Legiti-
"mate Monarchy was, to my Mind, the
"Rock over which the brawling River
"leaped awhile, and which, in the End,
"successfully opposed it; and as to your
"*Oliver*, he was a cunning Fellow, that
"diverted its Course to turn his own
"Mill."

"They that can see any Virtue or
"Comeliness in a *Charles Stuart*," says
Father, "can hardly be expected to
"acknowledge the rugged Merits of a
"plain Republican."

"Plain was the very last Thing he
"was," says Uncle, "either in speaking
"or dealing. He was as cunning as a
"Fox, and as rough as a Bear."

"We can overlook the Roughness of
"a good Man," says Father; "and if
"a

"a Temper subject to hasty Ebullitions
"is better than one which, by Blows and
"hard Usage, has been silenced into Sul-
"lenness, a Republic is better than an
"absolute Sovereignty."

"Aye; and if a Temper under the
"Control of Reason and Principle," rejoins Uncle, "is better than one unaccus-
"tomed to restrain its hasty Ebullitions,
"a limited Monarchy is better than a
"Republic."

"But ours is not limited enough," persists Father.

"Wait awhile," returns Uncle, "till, as
"you say, we have filtered over the
"Gravel a little longer, and then see
"how clear we shall run."

"I don't see much present Chance of
"it," says Father. "Such a King, and
"such a Court!"

"The King and Court will soon shift
"Quarters, I understand," says Uncle;
"for Fear of this coming Sickness.
"'Twould be a rare Thing, indeed, for
"the King to take the Plague!"

"Why

" Why not the King, as well as any of
" his Commons?" says Father. "Tush!
" I am tired of the Account People make
" of him. 'Is *Philip* dead?' 'No; but
" he is sick.' Pray, what is it to us,
" whether *Philip* is sick or not?"

"Which of the *Phillipses*, my Dear?"
asks Mother. "Did you say *Jack Phil-
" lips* was sick?"

"No, dear *Betty*; only a King of
" *Macedon*, who lived a long Time ago."

"Doctor *Brice* commends you much
" for your grounding the *Phillipses* so ex-
" cellently in the Classicks," says Uncle.

"He should think whether his Praise
" is much worth having," says Father,
rather haughtily. "The young Men were
" indebted to me for a competent Know-
" ledge of the learned Tongues—no more."

"Nay, somewhat more," rejoined Uncle;
" and the Praise of a worthy Man is surely
" always worth having."

"If he be our Superior in the Thing
" wherein he praises us," returned Father.
" His Praise is then a Medal of Reward;
" but

"but it should never be a current Coin, "bandied from one to another. And the "Inferior may never praise the Superior."

Uncle was silent a Moment, and then softly uttered, "My Soul, praise the Lord."

"There you have me," says Father, instantly softening. "Laud we the Name of "the Lord, but let's not laud one another."

"Ah! I can't wait to argue the "Point," says Uncle. "I must back to "the *Temple*."

"Stay a Moment, *Kit*. Have you seen "'the Mysterie of Jesuitism'?"

"No; have *you* seen the Proof that "*London*, not *Rome*, is the City on seven "Hills? *Ludgate Hill, Fish-street Hill,* "*Dowgate Hill, Garlick Hill, Saffron Hill,* "*Holborn Hill*, and *Tower Hill*. Clear as "Day!"

"Where's *Snow Hill?* Come, don't "go yet. We will fight over some of "our old Feuds. There will be a roast "Pig on Table at one o'Clock, and, I "fancy, a Tansy-pudding."

"*I* can't fancy Tansy-pudding," says Uncle,

Uncle, shuddering; "I cannot abide "Tansies, even in Lent. Besides, I'm "expecting a Reference."

"Oh! very well; then drop in again "in the Evening, if you will; and very "likely you will meet *Cyriack Skinner*. "And you shall have cold Pig for Supper, "not forgetting the Currant-sauce, *Wilt-* "*shire* Cheese, Carraways, and some of "your own Wine."

"Well, that sounds good. I don't "mind if I do," says Uncle; "but don't "expect me after nine."

"I'm in Bed by nine," says Father.

"Oh, oh!" says Uncle; and with a comical Look at us, he went off.

UNCLE *Kit* did not come last Night; I did not much expect he woulde; nor Mr. *Skinner*. Insteade, we had Dr. *Paget*, and one or two others, who talked dolefully alle the Evening of Signs of the Times,

Times, till they gave me the Horrors. One had seen a Ghost, or at least, seen a Crowd looking at a Ghost, or for a Ghost, in *Bishopgate* Churchyard, that comes out and points hither and thither at future Graves. Another had seene an Apparition, or Meteor, somewhat of human or angelic Shape, in the Air. Father laught at the first, but did not so discredit *in toto* the other; observing that *Theodore Beza* believed at one Time in astrologick Signs; and thought that the Appearance of the notable Star in *Cassiopeia* betokened the universal End. And as for Angels, he sayd they were, questionless, ministering Spiritts, not onlie sent forth to minister unto the Heirs of Salvation, but sometimes Instruments of God's Wrath, to execute Judgments upon ungodly Men, and convince them of the ill Deeds which they have ungodly committed; as during the Pestilence in *David's* Time, when the King saw the Destroying Angel standing between Heaven and Earth, having a drawn Sword in his Hand,

Hand, stretched over Jerusalem. Such Delegates we might, without Fanaticism, suppose to be the generall, though unseen, Instruments of public Chastisements; and, for our particular Comfort, we had equall Reason to repose on the Assurance, that even amid the Pestilence that walked in Darkness, and the Destruction that wasted by Noon-day, the Angels had charge over each particular Believer, to keep them in all their Ways. Adding, that, though he forbore, with *Calvin*, to pronounce that each Man had his own Guardian Spiritt,— a Subject whereon Scripture was silent,— we had the Lord's own Word for it, that little Children were the particular Care of holy Angels.

And this, and othermuch to same Purport, had soe soothing and sedative an Effect, that we might have gone to Bed in peacefull Trust, onlie that Dr. *Paget* must needs bring up, after Supper, the correlative Theme of the great *Florentine* Plague, and the poisoned Wells, which sett Father off upon the Acts of Mercy
of

of Cardinal *Borromeo*,—not him called St. *Charles*, but the Cardinal-Archbishop,— and soe, to the Pestilence at *Geneva*, when even the Bars and Locks of Doors were poisoned by a Gang of Wretches, who thought to pillage the Dwellings of the Dead; till we all went to Bed, moped to Death.

Howbeit, I had been warmly asleep some Hours, (more by Token I had read the ninety-first Psalm before getting into Bed), when *Anne*, clinging to me, woke me up with a shrill Cry. I whispered fearfullie, " What is't ?—a Thief under " the Bed ? "

" No, no," she replies. " Listen ! "

Soe I did for a While; and was just going to say, " You were dreaming," when a hollow Voice in the Street, beneath our Window, distinctlie proclaimed,

" Yet forty Days, and *London* shall be " destroyed ! I will overturn, overturn, " overturn it ! Oh ! Woe, Woe, Woe ! "

I sprang out of Bed, fell over my Shoes, got up again, and ran to the Window. There

There was Nothing to be seen but long,

black Shadows in the Streets. The Moon was behind the House. After looking
forthe

s

forthe awhile, with Teeth chattering, I was about to drop the Curtain, when, afar off, whether in or over some distant Quarter of the Town, I heard the same Voice, clearlie enow to recognise the Rhythm, though not the Words. I crept to Bed, chilled and awe-stricken; yet, after cowering awhile, and saying our Prayers, we both fell asleep.

THE first Sounde this Morning was of Weeping and Wayling. Mother had beene scared by the Night-warning, and wearied Father to have us alle into the Countrie. He thought the Danger not yet imminent, the Expense considerable, and the Outcry that of some crazy Fanatick; ne'erthelesse, consented to employ *Ellwood* to look us out some country Lodgings; having noe Mind to live upon my Uncle at *Ipswich*.

Mary, strange to say, had heard noe Noise;

Noise; nor had the Maids; but Servants always sleep heavily.

Some of the Pig having beene sett aside for my Uncle, and Mother fancying it for her Breakfast, was much putt out, on going into the Larder, to find it gone. *Betty*, of course, sayd it was the Cat. Mother made Answer, she never knew a Cat partiall to cold Pig; and the Door having been latched, was suspicious of a Puss in Boots.

Betty cries—" Plague take the Cat!"

Mother rejoyns—" If the Plague does " not take him, I shall certainly have " him hanged."

" Then we shall be overrun with Rats," says *Betty*.

" I shall buy Ratsbane for them," says Mother; and soe into the Parlour, where Father, having hearde the whole Dialogue, had been greatlie amused.

At Twilight, she went to look at the Pantry Fastenings herselfe, but, suddenlie hearing a dolorous Voyce either within or immediately without, cry, " Oh! Woe, " Woe!"

"Woe!" she naturallie drew back. However, being a Woman of much Spiritt, she instantlie recovered herselfe, and went forward; but no one was in the Pantry. The Occurrence, therefore, made the more Impression; and she came up somewhat scared, and asked if we had heard it.

"My Dear," says Father, "you awoke
" me in the midst of a very interesting
" Colloquy between *Sir Thomas More* and
" *Erasmus.* However, I think a Dog
" barked, or rather howled, just now.
" Are you sure the words were not 'Bow,
" wow, wow'?"

NOTHER Night-larum; but onlie from Father, who wanted me to write for him,—a Task he has much intromitted of late. Mother was hugelie annoyed at it, and sayd,—"My Dear, I am per-
" suaded that if you would not persist in
" going to Bed soe earlie, you woulde not
" awake at these untimelie Hours."

"That

"That is very well for you to say," returned he, "who can sew and spin the "whole Evening through; but I, whose "long entire Day is Night, grow soe tired "of it by nine o'Clock, that I am fit for "Nothing but Bed."

"Well," says she, "I often find that "brushing my Hair wakes me up when "I am drowsy. I will brush yours To-"Morrow Evening, and see if we cannot "keep you up a little later, and provide "sounder Rest for you when you do turn "in."

Soe, this Evening, she casts her Apron over his Shoulders, and commences combing his Hair, chatting of this and that, to keep him in good Humour.

"What beautiful Hair this is of yours, "my Dear!" says she; "soe fine, long, "and soft! scarcelie a Silver Thread in "it. I warrant there's manie a young "Gallant at Court would be proud of "such."

"Girls, put your Scissars out of your "Mother's Way," says Father; "she's a
"perfect

"perfect *Dalilah*, and will whip off Half my Curls before I can count Three, unless you look after her. And I," he adds, with a Sigh, "am, in one Sort, a *Samson*."

"I'm sure *Dalilah* never treated *Samson's* old Coat with such Respect," says Mother, finishing her Task, resuming her Apron, and kissing him. "Soe now, keep your Eyes open—I mean, keep awake, till I bring you a Gossip's Bowl."

When she was gone, Father continued sitting bolt upright, *his Eyes*, as she sayd (his beautiful Eyes!), open and wakefull, and his Countenance composed, yet grave, as if his Thoughts were at least as far off as *Tangrolipix* the *Turk*. All at once, he says,

"*Deb*, are my Sleeves white at the Elbow?"

"No, Father."

"Or am I shiny about the Shoulders?"

"No, Father."

"Why, then," cries he, gaily, "this Coat can't

"can't be very old, however long I may
"have worn it. I'll rub on in it still;
"and your Mother and you will have
"the more Money for copper-coloured
"Clokes. But don't, at any Time, let
"your Father get shabby, Children. I
"would never be threadbare nor unclean.
"Let my Habitt be neat and spotless, my
"Bands well washed and uncrumpled, as
"becometh a Gentleman. As for my
"Sword in the Corner, your Mother may
"send that after my Medal as soon as she
"will. The *Cid* parted with his *Tizona*
"in his Life-time; soe a peaceable Man,
"whose Eyes, like the Prophet *Abijah's*,
"are set, may well doe the same."

May 12.

YESTERDAY being the *Lord's Day*, Mother was hugely scared during Morning Service, by seeing an old Lady put her Kerchief to her Nose, look hither and thither, and, finally, walk out of of Church. One whispered another, "A "Plague-Smell, perchance." "No Doubt "on't;" and soe, one after another left, as, at length, did Mother, who declared she beganne to feel herself ill. On the Cloth being drawn after Dinner, she made a serious Attack on my Father, upon the Subject of Country Lodgings, which he stoutly resisted at first, saying,

"If, Wife and Daughters, either the "Danger were so immediate, or the Es-"cape from it so facile as to justify these "womanish Clamours, Reason would that "I should listen to you. But, since that "the Lord is about our Bed, and about "our Path, in the Capital no less than "in the Country, and knoweth them that "are his, and hideth them under the "Shadowe of his Wings—and since that, "if the Fiat be indeed issued agaynst us, "no Stronghold, though guarded with "triple Walls of Circumvallation, like *Ec-*"*batana,* nor pastoral Valley, that might "inspire *Theocritus* with a new Idyl, can "hide us, either by its Strength or its
"Obscurity,

"Obscurity, from the Arrow of the Destroying Angel; ye, therefore, seeing these Things cannot be spoken agaynst, ought to be quiet, and do Nothing rashly. Wherefore, I pray you, Wife and Daughters, get you to your Knees, before Him who alone can deliver you from these Terrors; and having cast your Burthen upon Him, eat your Bread in Peacefulness and Cheerfulness of Heart."

However, we really are preparing for Country Quarters, for young *Ellwood* hath this Morning brought us Note of a rustick Abode near his Friends, the *Penningtons*, at *Chalfont*, in *Bucks*, the Charges of which suit my Father's limited Means; and we hope to enter on it by the End of the Week. *Ellwood's* Head seems full of *Guli Springett*, the Daughter of Master *Pennington's* Wife by her first Husband. If Half he says of her be true, I shall like to see the young Lady. We part with one Maid, and take the other. *Betty* was very forward to be left in Charge; and

and profest herself willing to abide any Risk for the Sake of the Family; more by Token she thoughte there was no Risk at alle, having boughte a sovereign Charm of Mother *Shipton*. Howbeit, on inducing her, much agaynst her Will, to open it, Nought was founde within but a wretched little Print of a Ship, with the Words, scrawled beneath it, " By " Virtue of the above Sign." Father called her a silly Baggage, and sayd, he was glad, at any Rate, there was no Profanity in it; but, in Spite of *Betty*, and *Polly*, and Mother too, he is resolved to leave the House under the sole Charge of Nurse *Jellycott*. Indeed, there will probably be more rather than less Work to do at *Chalfont;* but Mother means to get a little Boy, such as will be glad to come for Threepence a-Week, to fetch the Milk, post the Letters, get Flour from the Mill and Barm from the Brewhouse, carry Pies to the Oven, clean Boots and Shoes, bring in Wood, sweep up the Garden, roll the Grass, turn the Spit,

draw

draw the Water, lift Boxes and heavy Weights, chase away Beggars and infectious Persons, and any little odd Matter of the Kind.

MOTHER has drowned the Cats, and poisoned the Rats. The latter have revenged 'emselves by dying behind the Wainscot, which makes the lower Part of the House soe unbearable, 'speciallie to Father, that we are impatient to be off. Mother, intending to turn *Chalfont* into a besieged Garrison, is laying in Stock of Sope, Candles, Cheese, Butter, Salt, Sugar, Raisins, Pease, and Bacon; besides Resin, Sulphur, and Benjamin, agaynst the Infection; and Pill Ruff, and *Venice* Treacle, in Case it comes.

As to Father, his Thoughts naturallie run more on Food for the Mind; soe he hath layd in goodlie Store of Pens, Paper, and Ink, and sett me to pack his Books. At

At first, he sayd he should onlie require a few, and good Ones. These were all of the biggest; and three or four Folios broke out the Bottom of the Box. So then Mother sayd the onlie Way was to cord 'em up in Sacking; which greatlie relaxed the Bounds of his Self-denial, and ended in his having a Load packed that would break a Horse's Back. Alsoe, hath had his Organ taken to Pieces; but as it must goe in two severall Loads, and we cannot get a bigger Wagon,—everie Cart and Carriage, large or little, being on such hard Duty in these Times,—I'm to be left behind till the Wagon returns, and till I've finished cataloguing the Books; after which *Ned Phillips* hath promised to take me down on a Pillion.

Nurse *Jellycott,* being sent for from *Wapping,* looked in this Forenoon, for Father's Commands. Such Years have passed since we lost Sight of her, that I remembered not her Face in the least, but had an instant Recollection of her chearfulle, gentle Voyce. Spite of her Steeple

Steeple Hat, and short scarlet Cloke, which gave her an antiquated Ayr, her cleare hazel Eyes and smooth-parted Silver Locks gave her an engaging Appearance. The World having gone ill with her, she thankfullie takes Charge of the Premises; and though her Eyes filled with Tears, 'twas with looking at Father. He, for his Part, spake most kindlie, and gave her his Hand, which she kissed.

THEY are all off. Never was House in such a Pickle! The Carpets rolled up, but the Boards beneath 'em unswept, and black with Dirt; as Nurse gladlie undertook everie Office of that Kind, and sayd 'twould help to amuse her when we were away. But she has tidied up the little Chamber over the House-door she means to occupy, and sett on the Mantell a Beau-pot of fresh Flowers she brought with her. The whole House smells

smells of aromatick Herbs, we have burnt soe many of late for Fumigation; and, though we fear to open the Window, yet, being on the shady Side, we doe not feel the Heat much.

Yesterday, while in the Thick of packing, and Nobody being with Father but me, a Messenger arrived, with a few Lines, writ privily by a Friend of poor *Ellwood*, saying he was in *Aylesbury* Gaol, not for Debt, but for his Opinions, and praying Father to send him twenty or thirty Shillings for immediate Necessaries. Mother having gone to my Lord Mayor for Passports, and Father having long given up to her his Purse, . . . (for us Girls, we rarelie have a Crown,) he was in a Strait, and at length said,

"This poor young Fellow must not be "denied. . . . A Friend in Need is a "Friend indeed. . . . Tie on thy Hood, "Child, and step out with the Volume "thou hadst in thy Hand but now, to "the Stall at the Corner. See *Isaac* him-"self; shew him *Tasso's* Autograph on
"the

"took the Volume to his Shop"

"the Fly-leaf, and ask him for thirty or "forty Shillings on it till I come back; "but bid him on no Pretence to part "with it."

I did so, not much liking the Job—there are often such queer People there; for old *Isaac* deals not onlie in old Books, but old Silver Spoons. Howbeit, I took the Volume to his Shop, and as I went in, *Betty* came out! What had been *her* Businesse, I know not; but she lookt at me and my Book as though she should like to know *mine;* but, with her usual demure Curtsey, made Way for me, and walked off. I got the Money with much Waiting, but not much other Difficultie, and took it to Father, who sent twenty Shillings to *Ellwood,* and gave me five for my Payns. Poor *Ellwood!* he hath good Leisure to muse now on *Guli Springett.*

MOTHER

OTHER was soe worried by the Odour of the Rats, that they alle started off a Day sooner than was first intended, leaving me merelie a little extra Packing. Consequence was, that this Morning, before Dawn, being earlie at my Task, there taps me at the Window an old Harridan that Mother can't abide, who is always a crying, " Anie Kitchen-stuff have you, " Maids ? "

Quoth I, " We've Nothing for you."

" Sure, my deary," answers she, in a cajoling Voyce, " there's the Dripping and " Candles you promised me this Morning, " along with the Pot-liquor."

" Dear Heart, Mrs. *Deb !* " says Nurse, laughing, " there is, indeed, a Lot of Kit- " chen-stuff hid up near the Sink, which " I dare say your Maid told her she was " to have; and as it will only make the " House smell worse, I don't see why she " should not have it, and pay for it too."

Soe

Soe I laught, and gave it her forthe, and she put into my Hand two Shillings; but then says, " Why, where's the " Cheese ? "

" We've no Cheese for you," sayd I.

" Well," says she, " it's a dear Bargayn ; " but . . ." peering towards me, "is t'other " Mayd gone, then ? "

" Oh, yes ! both of 'em," says I ; " and " I'm the Mistress," soe burst out a laughing, and shut the Window, while she stumped off, with Something between a Grunt and a Grone. Of course, I gave the Money to Nurse.

We had much Talk overnight of my poor dear Mother. Nurse came to her when *Anne* was born, and remained in the Family till after the Death of Father's second Wife. *She* was a fayr and delicate Gentlewoman, by Nurse's Account, soft in Speech, fond of Father, and kind to us and the Servants ; but all Nurse's Suffrages were in Favour of mine own loved Mother.

I askt Nurse how there came to have beene

beene a Separation betweene Father and Mother, soone after their Marriage. She made Answer, she never could understand the Rights of it, having beene before her Time; but they were both so good, and tenderly affectioned, she never could believe there had beene anie reall Wrong on either Side. She always thought my Grandmother must have promoted the Misunderstanding. Men were seldom fond of their Mothers-in-law. He was very kind to the whole Family the Winter before *Anne* was born, when, but for him, they would not have had a Roof over their Heads. Old Mr. *Powell* died in this House, the very Day before *Christmas*, which cast a Gloom over alle, insomuch that my Mother would never after keep *Christmas Eve*; and, as none of the Puritans did, they were alle of a Mind. My other Grandfather dropt off a few Months after; he was very fond of Mother. At this time Grandmother was going to Law for her Widow's Thirds, which were little worth the striving for, except to One soe extreme

extreme poor. Yet, spite of Gratitude and Interest, she must quarrel with Father, and remove herself from his House; which even her own Daughter thought very wrong. Howbeit, Mother would have her first Child baptized after her; and sent her alle the little Helps she could from her owne Purse, from Time to Time, with Father's Privity and Concurrence. He woulde have his next Girl called *Mary*, after Mother; though the Name *she* went by with him was "Sweet "*Moll;*"—'tis now always "Poor *Moll*," or "Your Mother." Her health fayled about that Time, and they summered at *Forest Hill*—a Place she was always hankering after; but when she came back she told Nurse she never wished to see it agayn, 'twas soe altered. Father's Sight was, meantime, getting worse and worse. She read to him, and wrote for him often. He had become *Cromwell's* Secretary, and had received the public Thanks of the Commonwealth. . . . Great as his Reputation was at Home, 'twas greater

greater Abroad; and Foreigners came to see him, as they still occasionally doe, from all Parts. My Mother not onlie loved him, but was proud of him. All her Pleasures were in Home. From my Birth to that of the little Boy who died, her Health and Spiritts were good; after that they failed; but she always tried to be chearfull with Father. She read her *Bible* much, and was good to the Poor. Nurse says 'twas almost miraculous how much Good she did at how little Cost, except of Forethought and Trouble; and all soe secretlie. She began to have an Impression she was for an early Grave, but did not seem to lament it. One Night, Nurse being beside her, awoke her from what she supposed an uneasie Dream, as she was crying in her Sleep; but as soone as she oped her Eyes, she looked surprised, and said it was a Vision of Peace. She thought the Redeemer of alle Men had been talking with her, Face to Face, as a Man talketh with his Friend, and that she had fallen at his Feet in grateful

grateful Joy, and was saying, "Oh! I "can't express . . . I can't express—"

About a Week after, she dyed, without any particular Warning, except a short Prick or two at the Heart. My Father was by. 'Twas much talked of at the Time, she being soe young.

Discoursing of this and that, 'twas Midnight ere we went to Bed.

Chalfont.

ARRIVED at last; after what a Journey! *Ned* had sent me Word Overnight to expect, this Forenoon, a smart young Cavalier, on a fine prancing Steed, with rich Accoutrements. Howbeit, Cousin is neither smart nor handsome; and, at the Time specifyde, there was brought up to the Door an old white Horse, blind of one Eye, with an aquiline Nose, and, I should think, eight Feet high. The Bridle

Bridle was diverse from the Pillion, which was finely embroidered, but tarnisht, with the Stuffing oozing out in severall Places. Howbeit, 'twas the onlie Equipage to be hired in the Ward, for Love or Money . . . so *Ned* sayd . . . And he had a huge Pair of gauntlett Gloves, a Whip, that was the smartest Thing about him, and a kind of Vizard over his Nose and Mouth, which, he sayd, was to prevent his being too alluring; but I know 'twas to ward off Infection. I had meant to be brave; and Nurse and I had brushed up the green camblet Skirt, but the rent Mother had made in it would show; however, Nurse thought that, when I was up she could conceal it with a Corking-pin. Thus appointed, *Ned* led the Way, saying, the onlie Occasion on which a Gentleman needed not to excuse himself to a Lady for going first, was when they were to ride a Pillion. Noe more jesting when once a-Horseback; for, after pacing through a few deserted Streets, we found ourselves amidst such a Medly of Carts, Coaches,

Coaches, and Wagons, full of People and Goods, all pouring out of Town, that *Ned* had enough to do to keep cleare of 'em, and of the Horsemen and empty Vehicles coming back for fresh Loads. Dear Heart! what jostling, cursing, and swearing! And how awfull the Cause! Houses padlocked and shuttered wherever we passed, and some with red Crosses on the Doors. At the first Turnpike 'twas worst of all—a complete Stoppage; Men squabbling, Women crying, and much good Daylight wasted. Howbeit, *Ned* desired me to keep my Mouth shut, my Eyes open, and to trust to his good Care; and, by Dint of some shrewd Pilotage, weathered the Strait; after which, our old Horse, whose Paces, to do him Justice, proved very easie, took longer Steps than anie other on the Road, by which Means we soon got quit of the Throng; onlie, we continuallie gained on fresh Parties,—some dreadfully overloaded, some knocked up alreadie, some baiting at the Roadside, and many of the poorer Sort erecting

erecting 'emselves rude Tents and Cabins under the Hedges. Soon I began to rejoyce in the green Fields, and sayd how sweet was the Air; and *Ned* sayd, "Ah!"—a Brick-kiln," and signed at one with his Whip. But I knew the Wind came t'other Way; and e'en Bricks are better than dead Rats.

Half-way to *Amersham* found *Hob Carter's* Wagon, with Father's Organ in't, sticking in the Hedge, without Man or Horse; and, by-and-by, came upon *Hob* himself, with a Party, carousing. *Ned* gave it him well, and sent him back at double-quick Time. 'Twas too bad. He had left Town overnight, and promised to be at *Chalfont* by Noon. I should have beene fain to keep him in Advance of us; howbeit, we were forct to leave him in the Rear; and, about two Miles beyond *Amersham*, we turned off the high Road into a country Lane, which soon brought us to a small retired Hamlet, shaded with Trees, and surrounded with pleasant Meadows and Orchards, which

was

was no other than *Chalfont*. There was Mother near the Gate, putting some fine Things to bleach on a Sweetbriar-hedge. *Ned* stopt to chat with her, and learn where he might put his Horse, while I went to seek Father; and soon found him, sitting up in a strait Chair, outside the Garden-door. Sayd, kissing him, " Dear Father, how is't with you? Are " you comfortable here?"

" Anything but that," replies he, very shortlie. " I am not in any Way at my " Ease in this Place. I can get no definite " Notion of what 'tis like, and what Notion " I have is unfavourable. To finish all, " they have stuck me up here, like a " Bottle in the Smoke."

" But here is a Cushion for you," quoth I, running in and back agayn; " and I " will set your Seat in the Sun, and out " of the Wind, and put your Staff within " Reach."

" Thanks, dear *Deb*. And now, look " about, Child, and tell me, with Pre- " cision, what the Place is like."

Soe

Soe I told him 'twas an irregular two-storied Tenement, parcel Wood, parcel Brick, with a deep Roof of old Tiles that had lost their Colour, and were curiouslie variegated with green and yellow Moss; and that the Eaves were dentilled, with Birds' Nests built in 'em, and a big Honeysuckle growing to the upper Floor; and there was a great and a little Gable, and a heavy Chimney-stack; a Casement of four Compartments next the Door, and another of two over it; four Lattice-windows at t'other End. In Front, a steep Meadow, enamelled with King-cups and Blue-bells; alongside the Gable-end, a Village Road, with deep Cart-ruts, and Hawthorn Hedges. Onlie one small Dwelling at hand, little better than a crazy Haystack; Sheep in the Field, Bees in the Honeysuckle; and a little rippling Rivulet flowing on continually.

"Why, now you have sett me quite "at Ease!" cries he, turning his bright Eyes thankfully towards the Sky. "I "begin to like the Place, and to bless
"the

" the warm Sun and pure Air. Ha ! so
" there is a rippling Rivulet, that floweth
" on continually ! . . . Lord, forgive me
" for my peevish Petulance . . . for for-

" getting that I could still hear the Lark
" sing her Morning Hymn, scent the
" Meadow-sweet and new-mown Hay,
" detect the Bee at his Industry, and the
" Woodpecker

"Woodpecker at his Mischief, discern the Breath of Cows, and hear the Lambs bleat, and the Rivulet ripple continually! Come! Let us go and seek *Ned*."

And, throwing his Arm about me, draws me to him, saying, "This is my best Walking-stick," and steps forward briskly and fearlessly.

Truly, I think *Ned* loves him as though he were his own Father; and, indeed, he hath scarce known any other. Kissing his Hand reverently, he says,—" Honoured *Nunks*, how fares it with you? Do you like *Chalfont*?"

"Indeed I do, *Ned*," responds Father heartily. "'Tis a little *Zoar*, whither I and my fugitive Family have escaped from the wicked City; and, I thank God, my Wife has no Mind to look back."

"We may as well go in now," says Mother.

"No, no," says Father; "I feel there is an Hour of Summer's Sunset still left.

"left. We will abide where we are, and
"keep as long as we can out of the Smell
"of your Soapsuds. . . . Let's sit upon
"the Ground."

"And tell strange Stories of the Deaths
"of Kings," says *Ned*, laughing.

"That was the Saying, *Ned*, of one
"who writ much well, and much amiss."

"Let's forgive what he writ amiss, for
"the Sake of what he writ well," says
Ned.

"That will I never," says Father. "If
"paltry Wits cannot be holy and witty
"at the same Time, that does not hold
"good with nobler Spiritts. . . . If it
"did, they had best never be witty at all.
"Thy Brother *Jack* hath yet to learn that
"Strength is not Coarseness."

Ned softly hummed—

"*Sweetest Shakspeare, Fancy's Child!*"

"Ah! you may quote me against my-
"self," says Father; "you may quote
"*Beza* against *Beza*, and *Erasmus* against
"*Erasmus*; but that will not shake the
                                    "eternal

"eternal Laws of Purity and Truth. But,
"mind you, *Ned*, never did anie reach a
"more lofty or tragic Height than this
"Child of Fancy; never did any repre-
"sent Nature more purely to the Life;
"and e'en where the Polishments of Art
"are most wanting in him, he pleaseth
"with a certain wild and native Ele-
"gance."

"And what have you now in Hand,
"Uncle?" *Ned* asks.

"*Firmianus Chlorus*," says Father. "But
"I don't find Much in him."

"I mean, what of your own?"

"Oh!" laughing; "Things in Heaven,
"*Ned*, and Things on Earth, and Things
"under the Earth. The old Story,
"whereof you have alreadie seen many
"Parcels; but, you know, my Vein ne'er
"flows so happily as from the autumnal
"to the vernal Equinox. Howbeit, there
"is Something in the Quality of this Air
"would arouse the old Man of *Chios* him-
"self."

"Sure," cries *Ned*, "you have less Need
"than

" than any blind Man to complayn, since
" you have but closed your Eyes on Earth
" to look on Heaven!'

Father paused; then, stedfastly, in Words I've since sett down, sayd :—

" *When I consider how my Light is spent,*
" *Ere half my Days, in this dark World and*
    wide,
" *And that one Talent, which is Death to hide,*
" *Lodged with me useless, though my Soul more*
    bent
" *To serve therewith my Maker, and present*
" *My true Account, lest He, returning, chide;*
" '*Doth God exact Day-labour, Light denied?*'
" *I fondly ask. But Patience, to prevent*
" *That Murmur, soon replies,—*' *God doth not need*
" *Either Man's Work, or his own Gifts. Who*
    best
" *Bear his mild Yoke, they serve him best. His*
    State
" *Is kingly; Thousands at his Bidding speed,*
" *And post o'er Land and Ocean without Rest,*
" *They also serve who only stand and wait.*'"

... We were all quiet enough for a while after this ... *Ned* onlie breathing hard, and squeezing Father's Hand. At length, Mother calls from the House, " Who

"Who will come in to Strawberries and Cream?"

"Ah!" says Father, "that is not an ill Call. And when we have discussed our neat Repast, thou, *Ned*, shalt touch the Theorbo, and let us hear thy balmy Voice. Time was, when thou didst sing like a young Chorister."

. . . Just as we were returning to the House, *Mary* ran forth, crying, "Oh, *Deb!* you have not seen our Cow. She has just been milked, and is being turned out, even now, to the Pasture. See, there she is; but all the Others have gone out of Sight, over the Hill."

Mother observed, "Left to herself, she will go, her own Calf speedily seeking."

"My Dear," says Father, "that's a Hexameter: do try to make another."

"Indeed, Mr. *Milton*, I know nothing of Hexameters or Hexagons either: 'tis enough for me to keep all straight and tight. Let's to Supper."

Anne had crushed his Strawberries, and mixed them with Cream, and now she put

put his Spoon into his Hand, saying, in jest, "Father, this is Angels' Food, you "know. I have pressed the Meath from "many a Berry, and tempered dulcet "Creams."

"Hush, you Rogue," says he; "*Ned* "will find us out."

"Is Uncle still at his great Work?" whispers Cousin to Mother.

"Indeed, I know not if you call it "such," she replies, in the same Undertone. "He hath given over all those "grand Things with hard Names, that "used to make him so notable abroad, "and so esteemed by his own Party at "Home; and now only amuses himself "by making the *Bible* a Peg to hang his "Idlenesse upon."

Sure what a Look *Ned* gave her! Fearful lest Father should overhear (for Blindness quickens the other Senses), he runs up to the Bookshelf, and cries, "Why, Uncle, you have brought down "Plenty of Entertainment with you! "Here are *Plato*, *Xenophon*, and *Sallust*, "*Homer*

"*Homer* and *Euripides*, *Dante* and *Petrarch*, "*Chaucer* and *Spenser*, . . . and . . . oh, "oh! you read Plays sometimes, though "you were so hard upon *Shakspeare*. . . . "Here's 'La Scena Tragica d'*Adamo* ed "*Eva*,' dedicated to the Duchess of *Man-* "*tua*."

"Come away from that Corner, *Ned*," says Father; "there's a Rat behind the "Books; he will bite your Fingers—I "hear him scratching now. You had "best attack your Strawberries."

"I think this sort will preserve well," says Mother. "*Betty*, in 'lighting from "the Coach, must needs sett her Foot on "the only Pot of Preserve I had left; "which she had stuffed under the Seat, "instead of carrying it, as she was bidden, "in her Hand."

"How fine it is, though," says Father, laughing, "to peacock it in a Coach now "and then! *Pavoneggiarsi in un Cocchio!* "Only, except for the Bravery of it, I "doubt if little *Deb* were not better off "on her Pillion. I remember, on my
"Road

"Road to *Paris*, the Bottom of the Ca-
"roche fell out; and there sate I, with
"*Hubert*, who was my Attendant, with
"our Feet dangling through. Even the
"grave *Grotius* laughed at the Accident."

"Was *Grotius* grave?" says *Ned*.

"Believe me, he was," says Father.
"He had had Enough to make him so.
"One feels taller in the Consciousness of
"having known such a Man. He was
"great in practicall Things; he was also
"a profound Scholar, though he made
"out the fourth Kingdom in *Daniel's*
"Prophecy to be the Kingdoms of the
"*Lagidæ* and the *Seleucidæ*; which, you
"know, *Ned*, could not possibly be."

Chatting thus of this and that, we idled over Supper, had some Musick, and went to Bed. And soe much for the only Guest we are like to have for some Months.

Anne told me, at Bed-time, of the Journey down. The Coach, she said, was most uncomfortable, Mother having so over-stuffed it. For her Share, she had a Knife-box under her Feet, a Plate-
basket

basket at her Back, a Bird-cage bobbing over her Head, and a Lapfull of Crockery-ware. Providentially, *Betty* turned squeamish, and could not ride inside, so she was put upon the Box, to the great Comfort of all within. Father, at the Outset, was chafed and captious, but soon settled down, improved the Circumstances of the Times, made Jokes on Mother, recalled old Journies to *Buckinghamshire*, and, finally, set himself to silent Self-communion, with a pensive Smile on his Face, which, as *Anne* said, let her know well enow what he was about. Arrived at *Chalfont*, her first Care was to make him comfortable; while Mother, *Mary*, and *Betty* were turning the House upside down; and in this her Care, she so well succeeded, that, to her Dismay, he bade her take Pen and Ink, and commenced dictating to her as composedly as if they were in *Bunhill Fields*. This was somewhat inopportune, for every Thing was to seek and to set in Order; and, indeed, Mother soon came in, all of a Heat, and sayd,

sayd, " I wonder, my Dear, you can keep
" *Nan* here, at such idling, when she has
" her Bed to make, and her Box to un-
" pack." Father let her go without a
Word, and sate in peacefull Cogitation all
the Rest of the Evening—the only Person
at Leisure in the House. Howbeit, the
next Time he heard Mother chiding—
which was after Supper—at *Anne*, for trying to catch a Bat, which was a Creature
she longed to look at narrowly, he sayd,
" My Dear, we should be very cautious
" how we cut off another Person's Plea-
" sures. 'Tis an easy Thing to say to
" them, ' You are wrong or foolish,' and
" soe check them in their Pursuit; but
" what have we to give them that will
" compensate for it? How many harm-
" less Refreshments and Refuges from sick
" or tired Thought may thus be destroyed!
" We may deprive the Spider of his Web,
" and the Robin of his Nest, but can never
" repair the Damage to them. Let us live,
" and let live; leave me to hunt my But-
" terfly, and *Anne* to catch her Bat."

OUR

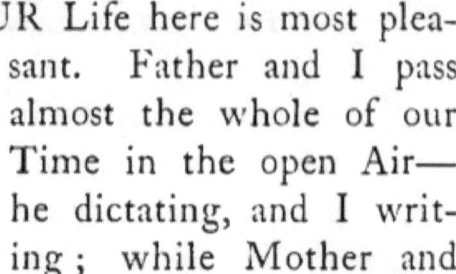UR Life here is most pleasant. Father and I pass almost the whole of our Time in the open Air— he dictating, and I writing; while Mother and *Mary* find 'emselves I know not whether more of Toyl or Pastime, within Doors,— washing, brewing, baking, pickling, and preserving; to say Nought of the Dairy, which supplies us with endless Variety of Country Messes, such as Father's Soul loveth. 'Tis well we have this Resource, or our Bill of Fare would be somewhat meagre; for the Butcher kills nothing but Mutton, except at *Christmass*. Then, we make our own Bread, for we now keep strict Quarantine, the Plague having now so much spread, that there have e'en been one or two Cases in *Chalfont*. The only One to seek for Employment has been poor *Anne*, whose great Resources at Home have ever been church-going and visiting poor Folk. She can do neither here,

here, for we keep close, even on the Sabbath; and she can neither read to Father, take long, lonely Rambles, nor help Mother in her Housewifery. Howbeit, a Resource hath at length turned up; for the lonely Cot (which is the only Dwelling within Sight) has become the Refuge of a poor, pious Widow, whose only Daughter, a Weaver of Gold and Silver Lace, has been thrown out of Employ by the present Stagnation of all Business. *Anne* picked up an Acquaintance with 'em shortly after our coming; and, being by Nature a Hoarder, in an innocent Way, so as always to have a few Shillings by her for charitable Uses, when *Mary* and I have none, she hath improved her Commerce with *Joan Elliott* to that Degree, as to get her to teach her her pretty Business, at the Price of the Contents of her little Purse. So these two sit harmoniously at their Loom, within Earshot of Father and me, while he dictates to me his wondrous Poem. We are nearing the End of it now, and have reached

reached the Reconciliation of *Adam* and *Eve*, which, I think, affected him a good deal, and abstracted his Mind all the Evening; for why, else, should he have so forgotten himself as to call me sweet *Moll?* . . . *Mary* lookt up, thinking he meant her; but he never calls her *Moll* or *Molly;* and, I believe, was quite unaware he had done so to me: but it showed the Course his Mind was taking.

This Morning, I was straying down a Blackthorn Lane, when a blue-eyed, fresh-coloured young Lady, in a sad-coloured Skirt, and large-flapped Beaver, without either Feather or Buckle, swept by me on a small white Palfrey. She held a Bunch of Tiger Lilies in her Hand, the gayety of which contrasted strangelie enow with her sober Apparell; and I wondered why a peculiar Classe of Folks should deem they please God by wearing the dullest of Colours, when He hath arrayed the Flowers of the Field in the liveliest of Hues. Somehow, I conceited her to be Mistress *Gulielma Springett*

Springett—and so, indeed, she proved; for, on reaching Home after a lengthened Ramble, I saw the Tiger Lilies lying on the Table, and found she had spent a full Hour with Father, who much relished her Talk. Sure, she might have brought a blind Man Flowers that had some Fragrance, however dull of hue.

To-day, as we were sitting under the Hedge, we heard a rough Voice shouting, "Hoy! hoy! what are you about "there?" To which another Man's Voice, just over against us, deprecatingly replied, "No Harm, I promise you, "Master.... We have clean Bills of "Health; and my Wife and I, Foot- "sore and hungry, do but Purpose to "set up our little Cabin against the "Bank, till the Sabbath is overpast."

"But you must set it up Somewhere "else," cries the other, who was the *Chalfont* Constable; "for we *Chalfont* "Folks are very particular, and can't "have Strangers come harbouring here
"in

"in our Highways and Hedges,—dying,
"and making themselves disagreeable."

"But we don't mean to die or be
"disagreeable," says the other. "We are
"on our Way to my Wife's Parish; and

"sure, you cannot stop us on the King's
"Highway."

"Oh! but we can, though," says the
Constable. "And, besides, this is not
"the King's Highway, but only a Bye-
"way, which is next to private Property;
"and

" and the Gentleman at present in Occu-
" pation of that private Property will be
" highly and justly offended if you go
" to give him the Plague."

"That's me," says Father. "Do tell
" him, *Deb*, not to be so hard on the poor
" People, but to let them abide where
" they are till the Sabbath is over. I
" dare say they have clean Bills of Health,
" as they state, and the Spot is so lonely,
" they need not be denied Fire and
" Water, which is next to Excommuni-
" cation."

So I parleyed with *John Constable*, and he parleyed with the Travellers, who really had Passports, and seemed Honest as well as Sound. So they were permitted, without Let or Hindrance, to erect their little Booth; and in a little while they had collected Sticks enough to light a Fire, the Smoke of which annoyed us not, because we were to Windward.

"What have we for Dinner To-day?" says Father.

"A

"A cold Shoulder of Mutton," says Mother, who had thrown 'em a couple of Cabbages.

"Well," says Father, "'twas to a cold "Shoulder of Mutton that *Samuel* set "down *Saul;* and what was good enough "for a Prophet may well content a Poet. "I propose, that what we leave of ours "To-day, should be given to these poor "People for their Sabbath's Dinner; and "I, for one, shall eat no Meat To-"day."

In fact, none did but *Mary* and Mother, who find fasting not good for their Stomachs; soe *Anne*, who is the most fearlesse of us all, handed the Joint over to them, with some broken Bread and Dripping, which was most thankfully received. In Truth, I believe them harmless People, for they are now a singing Psalms.

LLWOOD has turned up agayn, to the great Pleasure of Father, who delights in his Company, and likes his Reading better than ours, though he *will* call Pater Payter. Consequence is, I have infinitely more Leisure, and can ramble hither and thither, (always shunning Wayfarers), and bring Home my Lap full of Flowers and Weeds, with rusticall Names, such as *Ragged Robin*, *Sneezewort*, *Cream-and-Codlins*, *Jack-in-the-Hedge*, or *Sauce-alone*. Many of these I knew not before; but I describe them to Father, and he tells me what they are. He hath finished his Poem, and given it *Ellwood* to read, in the most careless Fashion imaginable, saying, "You can take "this Home, and run through it at your "Leisure. I should like to hear your "Judgment on it some Time or other." Nor do I believe he has ever since given himself an uneasy Thought of what that Judgment

Judgment may be, nor what the World at large may think of it. His Pleasure is not in Praise but Production; the last makes him now and then a little feverish; the other, or its want, never. Just at last, 'twas hard Work to us both; he was like a Wheel running downhill, that must get to the End before it stopped. Mother scolded him, and made him promise he would leave off for a Week or so; at least, she says he did, and he says he did not, and asks her whether, if the Grass had promised not to grow she would believe it.

Poor *Ellwood's* Love-bonds prove rather more irksome to him than those of his Gaol; he hath renewed his Intercourse with our Friends at the *Grange*, only to find a dangerous Rival stept into his Place, in the Person of one *William Penn*—in fact, I suspect Mistress *Guli* is engaged to him already. *Ellwood* hath been closetted with my Father this Morning, pouring out his Woes—methinks he must have been to seek for a Confidant! When he came

"he pours forth the full tide of Melody on his Organ"

came forth, the poor young Man's Eyes were red. I cannot but pity him, tho' he is such a Formalist.

I wish *Anne* were a little more demonstrative; Father would then be as assured of her Affection as of mine, and treat her with equal Tenderness. But, no, she cannot be; she will sitt and look piteously on his blind Face, but, alas! he cannot see that; and when he pours forth the full Tide of Melody on his Organ, and hymns mellifluous Praise, the Tears rush to her Eyes, and she is oft obliged to quit the Chamber; but alas! he knows not that. So he goes on, deeming her, I fear me, stupid as well as silent, indifferent as well as infirm.

I am not avised of her ever having let him feel her Sympathy, save when he was inditing to me his third Book, while she sate at her Sewing. 'Twas at these lines:—

"*Thus with the Year,*
"*Seasons return; but not to me returns*
"*Day, or the sweet Approach of Even or Morn,*
"*Or*

"*Or Sight of vernal Bloom or Summer's Rose,*
"*Or Flocks or Herds, or human Face divine,*
"*But Clouds instead, and ever-during Dark*
"*Surrounds me; from the cheerful Ways of
   Men*
"*Cut off: and for the Book of Knowledge fair,*
"*Presented with an universal Blank."*

His Brow was a little contracted, but his Face was quite composed; while she, on t'other Hand, with her Work dropped from her Lap, and her Eyes streaming, sate gazing on him, the Image of Woe. At length, timidly stole to his Side, and, after hesitating awhile, kissed both his Eyelids. He caught her to him, quite taken by Surprise, and, for a Moment, both wept bitterly. This was soon put a Stop to, by Mother's coming in, with her Head full of stale Fish; howbeit Father treated *Anne* with uncommon Tenderness all that Evening, calling her his sweet *Nan;* while she, shrinking back again into her Shell, was shyer than ever. But his Spiritts were soothed rather than dashed by this little Outbreak; and at Bedtime, he said, even cheerfully, " Now, good-
" night

" night, Girls : . . . may it, indeed, be
" as good to you as to me. You know,
" Night brings back my Day—*I am not
" blind in my Dreams.*"

I WISH I knew the Distinction between Temperament and Genius : how far Father's even Frame is attributable to one or t'other. If to the former, why, we might hope to attain it as well as he ; yet, no ; this is equallie the Gift of God's Grace. Our Humours we may controwl, but our Temperament is born with us ; and if one should say, " Why
" are you a Vessel of glorious things,
" while I am a Vessel of Things weak
" and vile ?"—nay, but oh ! Man or Woman, who art thou that questionest the Will of God? His Election is shewn no less in the Gift of Genius or of an equable Temperament than of spirituall Life ; and the Thing formed may not say to

to him that formed it, " Why hast thou " made me thus ? "

Father, indeed, can flame out in political Controversy, and lay about him as with a Flail, right and left, making the Chaff, and sometimes the Wheat too, fly about his Ears. 'Twas while threshing the Wheat by the Wine-press at *Ophrah*, that *Gideon* was called by the Angel; and methinks Father hath in like Manner been summoned from the Floor of his Threshing, to discourse of Heaven and Earth, and bring forth from his Mind's Storehouse Things new and old. I wonder if the World will ever give heed to his Teaching. Suppose a Spark of Fire should drop some Night on the Manuscript, while *Ellwood* is dozing over it; —why, there's an end on't. I suppose Father could never do it over again. I wonder how many fine Things have been lost in suchlike Ways; or whether God ever permitts a truly fine Thing to be utterly lost. We may drop a Diamond into the Sea; but there it is, at the bottom

bottom of the Great Deep. *Justinian's Pandects* turned up again. The Art of making Glass was lost once. The Passage round the *Cape* was made and forgotten. ——If I pore over this, I shall puzzle my Head. Howbeit, were I to round the *Cape*, I should hardly look for stranger and more glorious Scenes than Father hath in his Poem made familiar to me. He hath done more for me than *Columbus* for Queen *Isabel*—hath revealed to me a far better *New World*. Now, I scarce ever look on the setting Sun, surrounded by Hues more gorgeous than those of the High-priest's Breast-plate, without picturing the Angel of the Sun seated on that bright Beam which bore him, Slope downward, beneath the *Azores*. And, in the less brilliant Hour, I, by Faith or Fancy, discern *Ithuriel* and *Zephon* in the Shade; and by their Side a third, of regal Port, but faded Splendour wan. A little later still, can sometimes hear the Voice of God, or, as I suppose, we might say, the Word of God, walking in the Garden.
Pneuma!

Pneuma! His Breath! His Spirit! How hushed and still! Then, the Night cometh, when no Man can work—when the young Lions, in tropical Climes, waking from their Day-sleep, seek their Meat from God. Albeit they may prowl about the Dwellings of His people, they cannot enter, for He that watcheth them neither slumbers nor sleeps. Moreover, heavenly Vigils relieve one another at their Posts, and go their Midnight Rounds; sometimes, singing (Father says), with heavenly Touch of instrumental Sounds, in full harmonic Number joined . . . yes, and Shepherds, once, at least, have heard them.

And then . . . and then Mother cries, " How often, *Deb*, shall I bid you lock " the Gate at nine o'Clock, and bring me " in the Key?"

GOOD

Sept. 2nd.

GOOD so! Master *Ellwood* hath brought back the MS. at last, and delivered his Approbation thereon with the Air of a competent Authority, which Father took in the utmost good part, and chatted with him on the Subject for some Time. Howbeit, he is not much flattered, I fancy, by the Quaker's pragmatick Sanction, qualifyde, too, as it was, to show his own Discernment; and when I consider that the major part of Criticks may be as little fitted to take the Measure of their Subject as *Ellwood* is of Father, I cannot but see that the gleaning of Father's Grapes is better than the Vintage of the Critick's *Abiezer*.

To wind up all, *Ellwood*, primming up his Mouth, says, "Thou hast found much " to tell us, Friend *Milton*, on *Paradise* " *Lost;*—now, what hast thou to tell of " *Paradise Regained?*"

Father

Father said nothing at the Time, but hath since been brooding a good deal, and keeping me much to the Reading of the *New Testament;* and I think my Night-work will soon begin again.

Ellwood's Talk was much of *Guli Springett*, whom I have seen sundry times, and think high-flown, in spight of her levelling Principles and demure Carriage. The Youth is bewitched with her, I think; what has a Woman to do with Logique? My Belief is, he might as well hope to marry the Moon as to win Mistress *Springett's* Hand; however, his Self-opinion is considerable. He chode Father this Morning for Organ-playing, saying he doubted its lawfullness. Oh, the Prigg!

I grieve to think *Mary* can sometimes be a little spightfull as well as unduteous. She is ill at her Pen, and having To-day made some Blunder, for which Father chid her, not overmuch, she rudely made Answer, "I never had a Writing-master." *Betty*, being by, treasured up, as I could see,

see, this ill-natured Speech : and 'twas unfair too ; for, if we never had a Writing-master, yet my Aunt *Agar* taught us ; and 'twas our own Fault if we improved no more. Indeed, we have had a scrambling Sort of Education ; but, in many respects, our Advantages have exceeded those of many young Women ; and among them I reckon, first and foremost, continuall Intercourse with a superior Mind.

If a Piece of mere Leather, by frequent Contact with Silver, acquires a certain Portion of the pure and bright Metal ; sure, the Children of a gifted Parent must, by the Collision of their Minds, insensibly, as 'twere, imbibe somewhat of his finer Parts. *Ned Phillips*, indeed, sayth we are like People living so close under a big Mountain, as not to know how high it is ; but I think we . . . at least, I do. And, whatever be our scant Learnings, Father, despite his limited Means, hath never grutched us the Supply of a reall Want ; and is, at this Time, paying *Joan Elliott* at a good Rate for perfecting

perfecting *Anne* in her pretty Work. I am sorry *Mary* should thus have sneaped him; and I am sorry I ever either hurt him—by uncivil Speech, or wronged him by unkind Thought. Poor *Nan*, with all her Infirmities, is, perhaps, his best Child. Not that I am a bad one, neither.

My Night-tasks have recommenced of late; because, as he says—

"*I suoi Pensieri in lui Dormir non ponno;*"

which, being interpreted, means, "His "Thoughts would let him and his Daugh- "ter take no rest."

12*th*.

I KNOW not that any one but Father hath ever concerned themselves to imagine the Anxieties of the blessed Virgin during her Son's forty Days' mysterious Absence. No wonder that

"*Within her Breast, tho' calm, her Breast, tho' pure,*
"*Motherly Fears got Head.*"

Father

Father hath touched her with a very tender and reverent Hand, dwelling less on her than he did on *Eve*, whom he with perfect Beauty adorned, onlie to make her Sin appear more Sad. Well, we know not ourselves; but methinks I should not have transgrest as she did, neither, for an Apple.

15th.

AND now I have transgrest about a Pin! O me! what weak, wicked Wretches we are! " Behold, how great " a Matter a little Fire " kindleth!" And the Tongue is a Fire, an unruly Member. Sure, when I was writing, at Father's Dictation, such heavy Charges against *Eve*, I privily thought I was better than she; and, sifting the Doings of *Mary* and *Anne* through a somewhat censorious Judgment, maybe I thought I was better than they. Alas! we know not our own selves. And so, dropping a Stitch in my Knitting,

Knitting, I must needs cry out—" Here,
" any of you . . . oh, Mother ! do bring
" me a Pin." My Sisters, as Ill-luck
would have it, not being by, cries she,
" Forsooth, Manners have come to a fine
" Pass in these Days ! Bring her a Pin,
" quotha ! " Instead of making answer,
" Well, 'twas disrespectful ; I ask your
" Pardon ; " I must mutter, " I see what
" I'm valued at—less than a Pin."

"*Deb*, don't be unduteous," says Father
to me. " Woulde it not have been better
" to fetch what you wanted, than strangely
" ask your Mother to bring it ? "

" And thereby spoil my Work," answered I ; " but 'tis no Matter."

" 'Tis a great Matter to be uncivil,"
says Father.

" Oh ! dear Husband, do not concern
" yourself," interrupts Mother; "the Girl's
" incivility is no new Matter, I protest."

On this, a Battle of Words on both
sides, ending in Tears, Bitterness, and my
being sent by Father to my Chamber till
Dinner. " And, *Deb*," he adds, gravely,
but

but not harshly, " take no Book with you, " unless it be your *Bible*."

Soe, hither, with swelling Heart, I have come. I never drew on myself such Condemnation before—at least, since childish Days; and could be enraged with Mother, were I not enraged with myself. I'm in no Hurry for Dinner-time; I cannot sober down. My Temples beat, and my Throat has a great Lump in it. Why was *Nan* out of the Way? Yet, would she have made Things better? I was in no Fault at first, that's certain; Mother took Offence where none was meant; but I meant Offence afterwards. Lord, have mercy upon me! I can ask Thy Forgiveness, though not hers. And I could find it in me to ask Father's too, and say, " I have sinned against Heaven, " and in thy . . . thy *Hearing!*" And now I come to write that Word, I have a Mind to cry; and the Lump goes down, and I feel earnest to look into my *Bible*, and more humbled towards Mother. And . . . what is it Father says?—

" *What*

" *What better can I do, than to the Place*
" *Repairing, where he judged me, there confess*
" *Humbly my Fault, and Pardon beg, with Tears*
" *Of Sorrow unfeign'd, and Humiliation meek?*"

. . . He met me at the very first Word. " I knew you would," he said. " I knew the kindest Thing was to send " you to commune with your own Heart " in your Chamber, and be still. 'Tis " there we find the Holy Spirit and Holy " Saviour in waiting for us; and in the " House where they abide, as long as " they abide in it, there is no Room for " *Satan* to enter. But let this Morning's " Work, *Deb*, be a Warning to you, not " thus to transgress again. As long as " we are in peaceful Communion among " ourselves, there is a fine, invisible Cob- " web, too clear for mortal Sight, spun " from Mind to Mind, which the least " Breath of Discord rudely breaks. You " owe to your Mother a Daughter's Reve- " rence; and if you behave like a Child, " you must look to be punisht like a " Child."

" I

"I am not a mere Baby, neither," I said.

"No," he replied. "I see you can make Distinction between *Teknia* and *Paidia*; but a Baby is the more inoffensive and less responsible Agent of the two. If you are content to be a Baby in Grace, you must not contend for a Baby's Immunities. I have heard a Baby cry pretty loudly about a Pin."

This shut my Mouth close enough.

"You are now," he added gently, "nearly as old as your Mother was when I married her."

I said, "I fear I am not much like her."

He said nothing, only smiled. I made bold to pursue:—"What was she like?"

Again he was silent, at least for a Minute; and then, in quite a changed Tone, with somewhat hurried in it, cried,—

"*Like the fresh Sweetbriar and early May!*
"*Like the fresh, cool, pure Air of opening Day . . .*
"*Like the gay Lark, sprung from the glittering
    Dew . . .*
"*An Angel! yet . . . a very Woman too!*"

And,

And, kicking back his Chair, he got up, and began to walk hastily about the Chamber, as fearlessly as he always does when he is thinking of something else, I springing up to move one or two Chairs out of his Way. Hearing some high Voices in the Offices, he presently observed, " A contentious Woman is like a
" continuall Dropping. *Shakspeare* spoke
" well when he said that a sweet, low
" Voice is an excellent Thing in Woman.
" I wish you good Women would recol-
" lect that one Avenue of my Senses being
" stopt, makes me keener to any Impres-
" sion on the others. Where Strife is,
" there is Confusion and every evil Work.
" Why should not we dwell in Peace, in
" this quiet little Nest, instead of render-
" ing our Home liker to a Cage of un-
" clean Birds ? "

*Bunhill Fields, London,
Oct.* 1666.

PEOPLE have phansied Appearances of Armies in the Air, flaming Swords, Fields of Battle, and other Images; and, truly, the Evening before we left *Chalfont*, methought I beheld the Glories of the ancient City *Ctesiphon* in the Sunset Clouds, with gilded Battlements, conspicuous far —Turrets, and Terraces, and glittering Spires. The light-armed *Parthians* pouring through the Gates, in Coats of Mail, and military Pride. In the far Perspective of the open Plain, two ancient Rivers, the one winding, t'other straight, losing themselves in the glowing Distance, among the Tents of the ten lost Tribes. Such are One's Dreams at Sunset. And, when I cast down my dazed Eyes on the shaded Landskip, all looked in Comparison, so black and bleak, that methought how

how dull and dreary this lower World must have appeared to *Moses* when he descended from *Horeb*, and to our Saviour, when he came down from the *Mount of Transfiguration*, and to St. *Paul*, when he dropt from the seventh Heaven.

What a Click, Click, the Bricklayers make with their Trowels, thus bringing me down from my Altitudes! Sure, we hardly knew how well off we were at *Chalfont*, till we came back to this unlucky Capital, looking as desolate as *Jerusalem*, when the City was ruinated and the People captivated. Weeds in the Streets—smouldering Piles—blackened, tottering Walls—and inexhaustible Heaps of vile Rubbish. Even with closed Windows, everything gets covered with a Coating of fine Dust. Cousin *Jack* Yesterday picked up a half-burnt Acceptance for twenty thousand Pounds. There is a fine Time coming for Builders and Architects—*Anne's* Lover among the Rest. The Way she picked him up was notable. Returning to Town,

Town, she falls to her old Practices of
daily Prayers and visiting the Poor. At
Church she sits over against a good-
looking young Man, recovered from the
Plague, whose near approach to Death's
Door had made him more godly in his
Walk than the general of his Age and
Condition. He notes her beautiful Face
—marks not her deformed Shape ; and,
because that, by Reason of the late Dis-
tresses, the Calamities of the Poor have
been met by unusuall Charities of the
upper Classes, he, on his Errands of
Mercy among the Rest, presently falls
in with her at a poor sick Man's House,
and marvels when the limping Stranger
turns about and discovers the beautiful
Votaress. After one or two chance
Meetings, respectfully accosts her—*Anne*
draws back—he finds a mutuall Friend
—the Acquaintance progresses ; and at
length, by Way of first Introduction to
my Father, he steps in to ask him (preamble supposed) to give him his eldest
Daughter. Then what a Storm ensues !
Father's

Father's Objections do not transpire, no one being by but Mother, who is unlikely to soften Matters. But, so soon as *John Herring* shuts the Door behind him, and walks off quickly, *Anne* is called down, and I follow, neither bidden nor hindered. Thereupon, Father, with a red Heat-spot on his Cheek, asks *Anne* what she knows of this young Man. Her answer, " Nothing but good." " How " came she to know him at all ? " . . . Silent ; then makes Answer, " Has seen " him at Mrs. *French's* and elsewhere." " Where else ? " " Why, at Church, and " other Places." Mother here puts in, " What other Places ? " . . . " Sure what " can it signify," *Anne* asks, turning short round upon her ; " and especially to you, " who would be glad to get quit of me " on any Terms ? "

" *Anne*, *Anne* ! " interrupts Father, " does this Concern of ours for you " look like it ? You know you are say- " ing what is uncivil and untrue."

" Well," resumes *Anne*, her breath coming

coming quick, "but what's the Objec-
"tion to *John Herring?*"

"*John?* is he *John* with you already?"
cries Mother. "Then you must know
"more of him than you say."

"Sure, Mother," cries *Anne*, bursting
into Tears, "you are enough to overcome
"the Patience of *Job*. I know nothing
"of the young Man, but that he is pious,
"and steady, and well read, and a good
"Son of reputable Parents, as well to do
"in the World as ourselves; and that he
"likes me, whom few like, and offers me
"a quiet, happy Home."

"How fast some People can talk when
"they like," observes Mother; at which
Allusion to *Anne's* Impediment, I dart
at her a Look of Wrath; but *Nan* only
continues weeping.

"Come hither, Child," interposes Father,
holding his Hand towards her; "and you,
"good *Betty*, leave us awhile to talk over
"this without Interruption." At which,
Mother, taking him literally, sweeps up
her Work, and quits the Room. "The
"Address

"Address of this young Man," says Father, "has taken me wholly by Surprise, and "your Encouragement of it has incontest- "ably had somewhat of clandestine in it; "notwithstanding which, I have, and can "have, nothing in View, dear *Nan*, but "your Well-being. As to his Calling, I "take no Exceptions at it, even though, "like *Cæmentarius*, he should say, I am a "Bricklayer, and have got my Living by "my Labour—"

"A Master-builder, not a Bricklayer," interposes *Anne*.

Father stopt for a Moment; then re- sumed. "You talk of his offering you a "quiet Home: why should you be dis- "satisfied with your own, where, in the "Main, we are all very happy together? "In these evil Times, 'tis something con- "siderable to have, as it were, a little "Chamber on the Wall, where your "Candle is lighted by the Lord, your "Table spread by him, your Bed made "by him in your Health and Sickness, "and where he stands behind the Door,
"ready

" ready to come in and sup with you.
" All this you will leave for One you
" know not. How bitterly may you
" hereafter look back on your present
" Lot! You know, I have the Apostle's
" Word for it, that, if I give you in
" Marriage, I may do well; but, if I
" give you not, I shall do better. The
" unmarried Woman careth for the Things
" of the Lord, that she may be holy in
" Body and Spirit, and attend upon him
" without Distraction. Thus was it with
" the five wise Maidens, who kept their
" Lamps ready trimmed until the Coming
" of their Lord. I wish we only knew
" of five that were foolish. Time would
" fail me to tell you of all the godly
" Women, both of the elder and later
" Time, who have led single Lives with-
" out Superstition, and without Hypocrisy.
" Howbeit, you may marry if you will;
" but you will be wiser if you abide as you
" are, after my Judgment. Let me not to
" the Marriage of true Minds oppose Im-
" pediment; but, in your own Case—"

"Father,

"Father," interrupts *Anne*, "you know
"I am ill at speaking; but permit me to
"say, you are now talking wide of the
"Mark. Without going back to the
"Beginning of the World, or all through
"the *Romish Calendar*, I will content me
"with the more recent Instance of your-
"self, who have thrice preferred Marriage,
"with all its concomitant Evils, to the
"single State you laud so highly. Is it
"any Reason we should not dwell in a
"House, because St. *Jerome* lived in a
"Cave? The godly Women of whom
"you speak might neither have had so
"promising a Home offered to them, nor
"so ill a Home to quit."

"What call you an ill Home?" says Father, his Brow darkening.

"I call that an ill Home," returns *Anne*, stoutly, "where there is neither Union
"nor Sympathy—at least, for my Share,
"—where there are no Duties of which
"I can well acquit myself, and where
"those I have made for myself, and find
"suitable to my Capacity and Strength,
"are

"are contemned, let, and hindered,—
"where my Mother-Church, my Mo-
"ther's Church, is reviled—my Mother's
"Family despised,—where the few Friends
"I have made are never asked, while
"every Attention I pay them is grudged,—
"where, for keeping all my hard Usage
"from my Father's Hearing, all the Re-
"ward I get is his thinking I have no
"hard Usage to bear—"

"Hold, ungrateful Girl!" says Father;
"I've heard enough, and too much. 'Tis
"Time wasted to reason with a Woman.
"I do believe there never yet was one
"who would not start aside like a broken
"Bow, or pierce the Side like a snapt
"Reed, at the very Moment most De-
"pendance was placed in her. Let her
"Husband humour her to the Top of her
"Bent,—she takes French Leave of him,
"departs to her own Kindred, and makes
"Affection for her Childhood's Home the
"Pretext for defying the Laws of God and
"Man. Let her Father cherish her, pity
"her, bear with her, and shelter her from
"even

"even the Knowledge of the Evils of the
"World without,—her Ingratitude will
"keep Pace with her Ignorance, and she
"will forsake him for the Sweetheart of
"a Week. You think Marriage the
"supreme Bliss: a good many don't find
"it so. Lively Passions soon burn out;
"and then come disappointed Expec-
"tancies, vain Repinings, fretful Com-
"plainings, wrathful Rejoinings. You
"fly from Collision with jarring Minds:
"what Security have you for more For-
"bearance among your new Connexions?
"Alas! you will carry your Temper with
"you—you will carry your bodily Infir-
"mities with you;—your little Stock of
"Experience, Reason, and Patience will
"be exhausted before the Year is out, and
"at the End, perhaps, you will—die—"

"As well die," cries *Anne*, bursting into Tears, "as live to hear such a Rebuke as "this." And so, passionately wringing her Hands, runs out of the Room.

"Follow after her, *Deb*," cries Father; "she is beside herself. Unhappy me!
"tried

"tried every Way! An *Œdipus* with no
"*Antigone!*"

And, rising from his Seat, he began to pace up and down, while I ran up to *Nan*. But scarce had I reached the Stair-head, when we both heard a heavy Fall in the Chamber below. We cried, "Sure, that "is Father!" and ran down quicker than we had run up. He was just rising as we entered, his Foot having caught in a long Coil of Gold Lace, which *Anne*, in her disorderly Exit, had unwittingly dragged after her. I saw at a Glance he was annoyed rather than hurt; but *Nan*, without a Moment's Pause, darts into his Arms, in a Passion of Pity and Repentance, crying, "Oh, Father, Father, for- "give me! oh, Father!"

"'Tis all of a Piece, *Nan*," he replies; "alternate hot and cold; every Thing for "Passion, nothing for Reason. Now all "for me; a Minute ago, I might go to "the Wall for *John Herring*."

"No, never, Father!" cries *Anne*; "never, dear Father—"

"Dark

"Dark are the Ways of God," continues he, unheeding her; "not only
"annulling his first best Gift of Light
"to me, and leaving me a Prey to daily
"Contempt, Abuse, and Wrong, but
"mangling my tenderest, most apprehen-
"sive Feelings—"

Anne again breaks in with, "Oh, Father,
"Father!"

"Dark, dark, for ever dark!" he went on; "but just are the Ways of God to
"Man. Who shall say, 'What doest
"Thou?'"

"Father, I promise you," says *Anne*,
"that I will never more think of *John*
"*Herring*."

"Foolish Girl!" he replies sadly; "as
"ready now to promise too Much, as
"resolute just now to hear Nothing.
"How can you promise never to think
"of him? I never asked it of you."

"At least I can promise not to speak
"of him," says *Anne*.

"Therein you will do wisely," rejoins Father. "My Consent having been
"asked

" asked is an Admission that I have a
" Right to give or withhold it; and, as
" I have already told *John Herring*, I shall
" certainly not grant it before you are of
" Age. Perhaps by that Time you may
" be your own Mistress, without even
" such an ill Home as I, while I live,
" can afford you."

"No more of that," says *Anne*, interrupting him; and a Kiss sealed the Compact.

All this Time, Mother and *Mary* were, providentially, out of the Way. Mother had gone off in a Huff, and *Mary* was busied in making some marbled Veal.

The rest of the Day was dull enough: violent Emotions are commonly succeeded by flat Stagnations. *Anne*, however, seemed kept up by some Energy from within, and looked a little flushed. At Bed-time she got the start of me, as usuall; and, on entering our Chamber, I found her quite undrest, sitting at the Table, not reading of her *Bible*, but with
her

her Head resting on it. I should have taken her to be asleep, but for the quick Pulsation of some Nerve or Muscle at the back of the Neck, somewhere under the right Ear. She looks up, commences rubbing her Eyes, and says, " My Eyes " are full of Sand, I think. I will give " you my new Crown-piece, *Deb*, if you " will read me to sleep without another " Word." So I say, "A Bargain," though without meaning to take the Crown ; and she jumps into Bed in a Minute, and I begin at the Sermon on the Mount, and keep on and on, in more and more of a Monotone ; but every Time I lookt up, I saw her Eyes wide open, agaze at the top of the Bed ; and so I go on and on, like a Bee humming over a Flower, till she shuts her Eyes ; but, at last, when I think her off, having just got to *Matthew*, eleven, twenty-eight, she fetches a deep sigh, and says, " I wish I could hear Him " saying so to me . . . ' Come, *Anne*, " unto me, and I will give you Rest.' " But, in fact, He does so as emphatically
" in

"in addressing all the weary and heavy-
"laden, as if I heard Him articulating,
"'Come, *Anne*, come!'"

POST SCRIPTUM.

Spitalfields, 1680.

A GENEROUS Mind finds even its just Resentments languish and die away when their Object becomes the unresisting prey of Death. Such is my Experience with regard to *Betty Fisher*, whose ill Life hath now terminated, and from whom, confronted at the Bar of their great Judge, Father will, one Day, hear the Truth. As to my Stepmother, Time and Distance have had their soothing Effect on me even regarding her. She is down in *Cheshire*, among her own People; is a hale, hearty Woman yet, and will very likely outlive me. If she looked in on me

me this Moment, and saw me in this homely but decent Suit, sitting by my clear Coal-fire, in this little oak-panelled Room, with a clean, though coarse Cloth neatly laid on the Supper Table, with Covers for two, could she sneer at the Spouse of the *Spitalfields* Weaver? Belike she might, for Spight never wanted Food; but I would have her into the Nursery, shew her the two sleeping Faces, and ask her, Did I need her Pity then?

Betty's Death, calling up Memories of old Times, hath made me somewhat cynical, I think. I cannot but call to Mind her many ill Turns. 'Twas shortly after the Rupture of *Anne's* Match with *John Herring*. Poor *Nan* had over-reckoned on her own Strength of Mind, when she promised Father to speak of him no more; and, after the first Fervour of Self-denial, became so captious, that Father said he heard *John Herring* in every Tone. This set them at Variance, to commence with; and then, *Mary* detecting *Betty* in certain Malpractices, Mother

Mother could no longer keep her, for
Decency's Sake; and *Betty*, in revenge,
came up to Father before she left, and
told him a tissue of Lies concerning us,
—how that *Mary* had wished him dead,
and I had made away with his Books and
Kitchen-stuff. I, being at *Hackney* at the
Time, on a Visitt to *Rosamond Woodcock*,
was not by to refute the infamous Charge,
which had Time to rankle in Father's
Mind before I returned; and *Mary* having lost his Opinion by previous Squabbles
with Mother and the Maids, I came back
only to find the House turned upside
down. 'Twas under these misfortunate
Circumstances that poor Father commenced his *Sampson Agonistes*; and, though
his Object was, primarily, to divert his
Mind, it too often ran upon Things
around him, and made his Poem the
Shadow and Mirrour of himself. When
he got to *Dalilah*, I could not forbear saying, " How hard you are upon Women,
" Father!"

" Hard?" repeated he; " I think I
" am

"am anything but that. Do you call me hard on *Eve*, and the Lady in *Comus?*"

"No, indeed," I returned. "The Lady, like *Una*, makes Sunshine in a shady Place; and, in fact, how should it be otherwise? For Truth and Purity, like Diamonds, shine in the Dark."

He smiled, and, passing his Hand across his Brow to re-collect himself, went on in a freer, less biting Spirit, to the Encounter with *Harapha* of *Gath*, in which he evidently revelled, even to making me laugh, when the big, cowardly Giant excused himself from coming within the blind Man's Reach, by saying of him, that he had need of much washing to be willingly touched. He went on flowingly to

"But take good Heed my Hand survey not thee;
"My Heels are fetter'd, but my Fist is free,"

and then broke into a merry Laugh himself; adding, a Line or two after,

"His Giantship is gone, somewhat crest-fallen;
"... there,

" . . . there, Girl, that will do for To-
" day."

Meantime, his greater Poem had come out, for which he had got an immediate Payment of five Pounds, with a conditional Expectance of fifteen Pounds more on the three following Editions, should the Public ever call for 'em. And truly, when one considers how much Meat and Drink One may buy for Twenty Pounds, and how capricious is the Taste of the critikal World, 'tis no mean Venture of a Bookseller on a Manuscript of which he knows the actual value as little as a Salvage of the Gold-dust he parts with for a Handful of old Nails. At all events, the Sale of the Work gave Father no Reason to suppose he had made an ill Bargain; but, indeed, he gave himself very little Concern about it; and was quite satisfied when, now and then, Mr. *Marvell* and Mr. *Skinner*, or some other old Crony, having waded through it, looked in on him to talk it over. Money, indeed, a little more of it, would have been

been often acceptable. Mother now began to pinch us pretty short, and lament the unsaleable Quality of Father's Productions; also to call us a Set of lazy Drones, and wonder what would come of us some future Day; insomuch that Father, turning the Matter sedately in his Mind, did seriously conclude 'twould be well for us to go forth for a While, to learn some Method of Self-support. And this was accelerated by an unhappy Collision 'twixt my Mother and me, which, in a hasty Moment, sent me, with swelling Heart, to take Counsel of Mrs. *Lefroy*, my sometime Playfellow *Rosamond Woodcock*, then on the Point of embarking for *Ireland;* who volunteered to take me with her, and be at my Charges; so I took leave of Father with a bursting Heart, not troubling him with an Inkling of my Ill-usage, which has been a Comfort to me ever since, though he went to the Grave believing I had only sought my own Well-doing.

We

We never met again. Had I foreseen it, I could not have left him. The next Stroke was to get away *Mary* and *Anne*, and take back *Betty Fisher*. Then the nuncupative Will was hatched up; for I never will believe it authentick — no, never; and Sir *Leoline Jenkins*, that upright and able Judge, set it aside, albeit *Betty Fisher* would swear through thick and thin.

Sure, Things must have come to a pretty Pass, when Father was brought to take his Meals in the Kitchen! a Thing he had never been accustomed to in his Life, save at *Chalfont*, by Reason of the Parlour being so small. And the Words, both as to Sense and Choice, which *Betty* put into his Mouth, betrayed the Counterfeit, by savouring overmuch of the Scullion. " God have Mercy, *Betty!* I see " thou wilt perform according to thy " Promise, in providing me such Dishes " as I think fit whilst I live; and when I " die, thou knowest I have left thee all !" Phansy Father talking like that! Were
I

I not so provoked, I could laugh. And he to sell his Children's Birthright for a Mess of Pottage, who, instead of loving savoury Meat, like blind *Isaac*, was, in fact, the most temperate of Men! who cared not what he ate, so 'twas sweet and clean; who might have said with godly Mr. *Ball* of *Whitmore*, that he had two Dishes of Meat to his Sabbath-dinner,— a Dish of hot Milk, and a Dish of cold Milk; and that was enough and enough. Whose Drink was from the Well;—often have I drawn it for him at *Chalfont!*— and who called Bread-and-butter a lordly Dish;—often have I cut him thick Slices, and brought him Cresses from the Spring! Well placed he his own Principle and Practice in the Chorus's Mouth, where they say,

"*Oh, Madness! to think Use of strongest Wines*
"*And strongest Drinks our chief Support of Health!*"

So that Story carries its Confutation with it: *Ned Phillips* says so, too. As to what

what passed, that *July* Forenoon, between him and Uncle *Kit*, before the latter left Town in the *Ipswich* Coach, and with *Betty Fisher* fidgetting in and out of the Chamber all the Time . . . he may, or may not have called us his unkind Children; for we can never tell what Reasons had been given him to make him think us so. That must stand over. How many human Misapprehensions must do the same! Enough that one Eye sees all, that one Spirit knows all . . . even all our Misdoings; or else, how could we bear to tell Him even the least of them? But it requires great Faith in the greatly wronged, to obtain that Calm of Mind, all Passion spent, which some have arrived at. When we can stand firm on that Pinnacle, *Satan* falls prone. He sets us on that dizzy Height, as he did our Master; saying, in his taunting Fashion,—

"*There stand, if thou canst stand; to stand upright*
"*Will ask thee Skill;*"

but the Moment he sees we can, down he

he goes himself!—falls whence he stood to see his Victor fall! This is what Man has done, and Man may do,—and Woman too; the Strength, for asking, being promised and given.

FINIS

BY THE SAME AUTHOR

In crown 8vo, with an Introduction by the Rev. W. H. HUTTON, B.D., and Twenty-five Illustrations by JOHN JELLICOE and HERBERT RAILTON, price 6s. cloth elegant, gilt top.

The Household of Sir Thos. More

SOME PRESS NOTICES

Spectator.—"A delightful book. . . . Twenty-five illustrations by John Jellicoe and Herbert Railton show off the book to the best advantage."

Graphic.—"A picture, not merely of great charm, but of infinite value in helping the many to understand a famous Englishman and the times in which he lived."

Literary World.—"A charming reprint. . . . Every feature of the pictorial work is in keeping with the spirit of the whole."

Scotsman.—"This clever work of the historical imagination has gone through several editions, and is one of the most successful artistic creations of its kind."

Glasgow Herald.—"An extremely beautiful reprint of the late Miss Manning's quaint and charming work."

Sketch.—"In the front rank of the gift-books of the season is this beautiful and very cleverly illustrated reprint of a work which has lasting claims to popularity."

Magazine of Art.—"The grace and beauty of the late Miss Manning's charming work, 'The Household of Sir Thomas More,' has been greatly enhanced by the new edition now put forth by Mr. John C. Nimmo. . . . This remarkable work is not to be read without keen delight."

Academy.—"It is illustrated cleverly and prettily, and tastefully bound, so as to make an attractive gift-book."

Liverpool Post.—"We welcome the tasteful reprint with its artistic illustrations by John Jellicoe and Herbert Railton, and its helpful introduction by the Rev. W. H. Hutton."

LONDON: JOHN C. NIMMO, 14 KING WILLIAM ST., STRAND.

BY THE SAME AUTHOR

In crown 8vo, with an Introduction by the Rev. W. H. HUTTON, B.D., and Twenty-six Illustrations by JOHN JELLICOE and HERBERT RAILTON, price 6s. cloth elegant, gilt top.

Cherry & Violet

A Tale of the Great Plague

SOME PRESS NOTICES

Athenæum.—"The late Miss Manning's delicate and fanciful little cameos of historical romance possess a flavour of their own. . . . The numerous illustrations by Mr. Jellicoe and Mr. Railton are particularly pretty."

Sketch.—"A beautiful book! is the verdict, and one to read and read again. A similar verdict is to be passed on the drawings with which Messrs. Herbert Railton and John Jellicoe have enriched this edition, for which the Rev. W. H. Hutton has written a sympathetic prefatory note."

Daily Chronicle.—"We cannot doubt that 'Cherry and Violet' in its present attractive form will gain many new readers and still delight the old."

British Review.—"'Cherry and Violet' is a tale of the early years of the Stuart Restoration, of the Plague, and of the Fire of London. It is told with all the grace and skill which characterises 'Mary Powell.' . . . The book is well worthy of the attention of every one to whom Miss Manning's name and writings are unknown."

Literary World.—"Nearly thirty illustrations by Mr. John Jellicoe and Mr. Herbert Railton enrich the volume, and materially help to make it a dainty and acceptable book for presentation purposes."

Scotsman.—"Charmingly illustrated. . . . The book is all the more valuable, too, for a genial and recommendatory introduction from the pen of the Rev. W. Hutton."

Magazine of Art.—"With such a work of fiction before her as Defoe's 'Journal of the Plague,' Miss Manning showed not only extraordinary courage, but even a touch of genius, in approaching a similar theme, and dealing with it charmingly and successfully. It is her own grace and charm which have rendered this book worth preserving, fit to place with others of our foremost women writers."

Public Opinion.—"It is an example of a pure and beautiful style of literature."

Saturday Review.—"A very well written tale of the Great Plague."

LONDON: JOHN C. NIMMO, 14 KING WILLIAM ST., STRAND.

www.ingramcontent.com/pod-product-compliance
Lightning Source LLC
Chambersburg PA
CBHW030542300426
44111CB00009B/830